LIFE, WARFARE, AND VICTORY

Life,
Warfare,
& Victory

BY

DANIEL W. WHITTLE

AUTHOR OF "MEMOIR OF P. P. BLISS" AND "SOUL-WINNING."

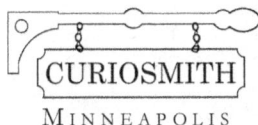

CURIOSMITH

MINNEAPOLIS

Published by Curiosmith.
P. O. Box 390293, Minneapolis, Minnesota, 55439.
Internet: curiosmith.com.
E-mail: shopkeeper@curiosmith.com.

Previously published by the Bible Institute Colportage Association in 1884.

Scripture verses are from *The Holy Bible*, King James Version.

Definitions are from *Webster's Revised Unabridged Dictionary*, 1828 and 1913.

ISBN 9781935626893

CONTENTS

PREFACE

his book has been prepared in the midst of Evangelistic work, to meet the wish often expressed to the writer—that instruction given in Bible Readings to young Converts might be made available for their more careful study and permanent use.

It is dedicated by the Author to those to whom he has preached Christ, in Great Britain as well as in America; as a token of his continued love for them and interest in their welfare: and is sent forth with the earnest prayer that the Holy Ghost may bless the study of the Scriptures it presents to them, and to all readers, for their spiritual growth and profit, and for the glory of our Lord Jesus Christ. To Him alone belongs all the praise for spiritual life and light, in both writer and reader, for "we are not sufficient of ourselves to think anything as of ourselves;"[1] and "the things of God knoweth no man but the Spirit of God."[2]

If the Spirit of God be honored and recognized as the Teacher, the Son of God will be revealed and magnified, and God the Father will delight to bless to the reader all of His own Word that shall be found herein.

1 2 Corinthians 3:5.
2 1 Corinthians 2:11.

Chapter 1

LIFE

He . . . cometh down from heaven, and giveth life unto the world.
—John 6:33.

The commencement of the Christian life is—LIFE: life imparted from God through Jesus Christ. "As many as received Him, to them gave He power to become the sons of God, even to them that believe on His name; which were born, not of blood, nor of the will of the flesh, nor of the will of man but of God" (John 1:12, 13). "This is life eternal, that they might know Thee, the only true God, and Jesus Christ, whom Thou hast sent" (John 17:3). "And this is the record, that God hath given to us eternal life; and this life is in His Son. He that hath the Son hath life; and he that hath not the Son of God hath not life" (1 John 5:11, 12).

It is vain to expect fruit unless the seed containing the fruit in germ has been *really sown*, and has taken *root*. It would be folly to look for anything but crab-apples from a crab-apple tree, if no better fruit had been grafted in upon its stem. So, it is useless to exhort a piety that does not exist, and fruitless to teach an unregenerate man to cultivate an unrenewed heart.

"That which is born of the flesh is flesh; and that which

is born of the Spirit is spirit" (John 3:6). Spiritual things may be imitated by, but cannot be produced from, the flesh. So at the very outset, in dealing with the subject of the soul's warfare, the question must be pressed home: "Have you been *born again?*" The spiritual difficulties of most professing Christians commence right here. They have not started right. The Gospel has not been clearly apprehended. Sincere in their desire to be Christians, believing the truths of the Bible, and more or less instructed in theology, they have given their public assent to these truths, made open profession of faith in Christ, and continued in the performance of religious duties, waiting for an inward evidence of their divine renewal, which has never come.

Now to all such the word must necessarily be, *Halt!* Go no further until this question is settled. Let us not consider the duties of the Christian life—its dangers or its delights—until we *have* the life. That it is the will of God that we *should* have life, is shown by the words of our Savior, "And this is the will of Him that sent Me, that every one which seeth the Son, and believeth on Him, should have everlasting life: and I will raise him up at the last day" (John 6:40). And that it is the will of God that those who believe should *know* that they have everlasting life—is us clearly shown by the words, "These things have I written unto you that believe on the name of the Son of God; that ye *may know* that ye have eternal life" (1 John 5:13). So from the Word of God itself it is made manifest, and would seem to go without saying, that I must know myself as a child of God, before I shall live as a child of God. Educating me to live like a child of God will not make me a child of God. It will only be an *imitation*, and must necessarily result in failure. The sooner those who are engaged in this imitation of Christian life in outward conduct, without real life in their souls, are brought to the knowledge of this, and realize that all in the past has been, and that all in the future will be, failure, upon that line—the sooner will their souls be brought to Him who is the Savior of *real* sinners, helpless to save themselves.

There are many illustrations in the Bible of the failure of all imitations of the life of faith. Saul the son of Kish, Israel's first king, forms a notable example. He was continually blundering in trying to act *like* a man of faith, but without possessing real faith. He evidently knew the Bible of his day; and had been instructed from it by Samuel, of God's dealings with Israel under Moses, Joshua, and the Judges (1 Samuel 12). So in his difficulties he tries to do what men of God had done before him—but never in the same spirit, or with the same results. In 1 Samuel 13:12 the Philistines are surrounding him. He evidently remembers Samuel's offering sacrifice and making prayer to God in a similar situation, as recorded in the seventh chapter; and although commanded by God in such circumstances to wait for the prophet, who would reveal God's will—he imitated Samuel, and offered sacrifice and made prayer. It was a mere outward form, an act of disobedience; of which, if he had been a man of faith he could not have been guilty; and disaster attended it. In 1 Samuel 14:18, remembering what the presence of the ark had been with Joshua at Jericho, he hastily commands the Priest to bring the ark: in the 19TH verse, he as hastily leaves Ark, Priest, and all, and goes out to the battle without *any* message from God; and in the 24TH verse blunders into another imitation of Joshua at Gibeon, by forbidding the people to eat food that day. He was disobeyed by his own son, and caused the people to sin by their eating blood. In the 35TH verse, in imitation of Gideon, he makes an altar; but no answer from God comes at this altar. In the 39TH verse, in imitation of Jephthah, he vows that Jonathan his son shall die; but the people will not allow Jonathan to be put to death, and the vow is broken. In the 41ST verse, without command from God, he again

imitates Joshua—who, by command of God, detected Achan by
the lot—in ordering the lot between himself and Jonathan. So
he blundered along, at times showing much courage and sincer-
ity of purpose; yet an Esau-man, a fine specimen of *the flesh*,
but without the faith of the living God to guide him. His life
of many failures closes with the creeping through the hut of the
Witch of Endor to a self-inflicted death upon the battle-field of
Gilboa. "Without faith it is impossible to please Him; for he that
cometh to God must believe that He is, and that He is a rewarder
of them that diligently seek Him" (Hebrews 11:6).

Saul was anointed and instructed by a prophet of God, and
was specially loved and prayed for by that prophet. He prayed,
and prophesied, and engaged in the service of God; and at times
with enthusiasm and courage. Yet, he was a man without faith,
and did not please God. "So then they that are in the flesh cannot please God" (Romans 8:8). These are solemn words; and the
example given is a solemn illustration of them.

Saul's lack of faith, was, *a failure to trust in the living God.*
It is not *faith* that saves; it is *God* that saves. God manifest to us
in Jesus Christ. "He that believeth on Him hath life."[1]

Saul's lack of faith in God, was shown by his disobedience of God. The sinner's lack of faith in God now, is shown
by disobeying God. The Gospel is preached among all nations
"for the obedience of faith" (Romans 16:26). "This is his com-
mandment, that we should believe on the name of his Son Jesus
Christ" (1 John 3:23). The notion that *faith* in and of itself has
any saving power or merit, apart from the object upon which
faith is placed, is a delusion. Yet many seem to think that if they
can force themselves to firmly believe the Bible, and never admit
any doubt of its contents, that a state of mind is produced that
constitutes *faith*, and that this state of mind is pleasing to God,

1 See John 3:36.

and that God on *account* of this state of mind forgives and saves them. And yet with this state of mind they are without personal trust in a personal Savior, and really put what they call *faith* in the *place* of their Savior.

Christ is the object of faith set forth in the scriptures. If I am not trusting in Him I have not saving faith, and am not saved any more than the heathen, who are not without faith (*i.e.* a firm belief in their superstitions), but *are* without the knowledge of the living God revealed in Jesus Christ. So, rejectors of the Gospel will often be heard saying, "Well, the Mohammedan has *his* belief, and the Hindoo *his* belief, and the Parsee *his* belief, and the Christian *his* belief. They all have *faith*, and each one who is sincere *in* his faith will be accepted of God." If *faith* simply saved, this might be so. But with the statement, "God hath given to us eternal life, and this life *is in His Son*. He that *hath the Son* hath life; and he that *hath not the Son, hath not* life," before us, its fallacy is readily seen. If a man puts faith in a real, living person, who has power to save him, and who engages to save him, he is certainly in a different position from the man who puts faith in that which has not life, and which is not truth.

There were those in the time of Noah who, undoubtedly, had firm belief, as the rain commenced falling, that the hills would be just as safe a refuge for them as the ark. Their firm belief made no difference in their fate. Noah had a firm belief in God's word, that the *ark* would save him. His belief led him to go into the ark, and the *ark*, not his belief, saved him.

So Christ is the alone object of faith; the ark into which, by believing in him, we enter and find salvation.

Most prayerfully and earnestly would the writer entreat all who may read these words to carefully ponder the testimony of God's Word in the chapter following, as to how we are born again, and what the evidences are that this New Birth has been experienced.

Chapter 2

DEATH BEFORE LIFE

From death to life.—JOHN 5:24; 1 JOHN 3:14.

ill the reader open his or her Bible at the Epistle to the Galatians, and carefully study some of the evidences there in a simple manner presented, as to how these Galatian Christians, to whom Paul had preached the Gospel, had been born again and made children of God. First, notice the third chapter, first and second verses. Four personalities are brought out: Jesus Christ, crucified; the Spirit of God imparted; Paul, the preacher of Christ; foolish Galatians, who had believed and rejoiced in believing, but were now being bewitched by legalists, who were getting their attention off from Christ. The point of connection between the Galatians and the truth preached, by which they received the Spirit, is emphasized in the simple words, "THE HEARING OF FAITH." Will the reader pause here, and ask what this means. Give a definition of it to your own mind without looking down the page. Put your hand over what follows until you think for yourself what the words *"the hearing of faith"* mean.

You have probably arrived at the same definition that would be ordinarily given—that it is, just believing what you hear.

Precisely so. It is the accepting as facts the statements of God's Word about oneself as a sinner, and about Christ as my Savior. "Faith cometh by hearing; and hearing by the *Word of God*" (Romans 10:17). This is a very important verse. Does the reader see its meaning? Faith does not come by *feeling*, but by *hearing;* and that hearing is not to be the hearing of man, be he the wisest and most eloquent that ever lived, but the hearing of the Word of God. The man is of use only as he *preaches* the Word, as did Paul at Galatia; the essence of the Word being *now*, as then, JESUS CHRIST CRUCIFIED. Faith is not a feeling; and feeling is not faith, and is not to be waited for before exercising faith. Faith is the trust of the mind or heart *in a person*, and is ordinarily brought into exercise by believing the words of that person. So John 5:24, "He that heareth my word, and believeth on Him that sent Me." (See also 1 Peter 1:25; John 1:12; James 1:18.) Following on now in Galatians, the attention of the reader is called to the opening up of the manner in which Paul preached Christ crucified, as developed from the 10TH to 14TH verses, inclusive, of the third chapter.

Some time ago, at an inquiry meeting, the writer met an inquirer who was brought into the light by a conversation over these verses; and he has often since used that conversation, with the illustration in it elaborated to meet special difficulties, to help others to apprehend Christ. Trusting that the use of it now may be owned of God to the same end, he proposes to produce it here. The man was an intelligent mechanic in middle life. When asked if he was saved, his reply was "No, I am not. I have been attending Gospel meetings for four weeks, and have been awakened to see that I am all wrong; but I cannot get light. I do not know how to become a Christian. I want to be saved, and am willing to do anything; but I do not know what to do." "Well, my friend," was the reply, "it is a great privilege to meet one in your state of mind, anxious about salvation, willing to be taught, and willing to yield to God. Now let us look for light where God has placed it—in His own Word. Will you read to me this verse (Galatians 3:10)." A Bible open at the passage was placed in his hand; and he read,

"For as many as are of the works of the law are under the curse: for it is written, Cursed is every one that continueth not in all things which are written in the book of the law to do them."

He looked a little surprised that such a verse should be pointed out to him as showing the way of salvation. Like all who seek salvation through Jesus Christ, he had first to see that he was *lost*, and *utterly lost*, before he could be *saved*; he had to learn that it is really and truly out of death that we are brought into life.

It is resurrection power that saves us; and resurrection power can only be shown where there is real death. So in the case of Lazarus, wherein the Son of God was to be glorified. Jesus tarried four days until Lazarus was dead; not sick merely, but dead. Then He came to Bethany; and resurrection power had the opportunity of manifestation. The dead one was made alive; the Son of God was glorified; and joy and gladness filled the home. Reader, is the blessing delayed in coming to you, because the Lord is waiting for you to see yourself dead: not sick merely with sin, but dead—condemned already under the curse of the broken law and without a spark of the life of God in your soul? There is one of two conditions for all: DEAD, or ALIVE. There is no middle ground.

Some questions came up on Galatians 3:10, with the man in the Inquiry Room. Let us listen to them:

"What does 'works of the law' mean?"

"Trying to keep the commandments of God."

"Well, is a man cursed for trying to do that?"

"No; but if he has chosen that as the way of salvation, and fails in keeping the commandments, then he is under the curse."

"What is the curse of the law?"

"Death, the penalty for disobedience. As in Ezekiel 18:4, 'The soul that sinneth it shall die;' and Romans 5:12, 'Death by sin;' and Romans 6:23, 'The wages of sin is death.'"

"Is every man who has not kept God's commandments under that penalty?"

"What does the verse say?"

"Well, it reads thus:

"'Cursed is every one that continueth not in all things which are written in the book of the law to do them.'"

"Well, my friend, have you continued doing all things commanded you by God?"

"No, I have not; and I am therefore under the curse. What can I do?"

"Well, what can you do? Supposing you should make a solemn vow tonight that you never, as long as you lived, would disobey God again; but that from this time forward you would faithfully observe all His commandments, and be perfectly pure in thought, deed, and life, before Him. Do you think you could keep such a vow, and never do a single wrong thing again?"

"No," said the man, sadly; "I don't think I could."

"No; and I don't think you could, either. And I am not going to ask you to make any such vow. But, supposing you did make it and did fulfil it, would a perfect life in the future atone for the disobedience of the past, and satisfy the penalty already due?"

"No, I don't think it would. If I owe my grocer twenty dollars on last year's account, my paying for all I get this year won't pay that."

"Well, my friend, your condition is certainly a solemn one. You confess that you have sinned; and the penalty for sin is death. It is not that you are going to be lost; but you are lost. Our Savior teaches this in John 3:18, where He says, 'He that believeth not is condemned *already.*' Do you see your position?"

"Yes, I do. I am under the curse. What must I do to be saved?"

"Under the Curse." Oh, solemn word!
   Lost soul, its truth be heeding:
From justice comes the dread award;
   For mercy be thou pleading.

"Under the Curse." It must be so;
   If sin I have been sharing:
God's wrath for sin I needs must know,
   The law must be unsparing.

"Under the Curse." A holy God
   Must give a law that's holy;
And justly then must keep His word,
   And punish sin most fully.

"Under the Curse." Oh, fearful doom!
   Oh, awful day that's nearing,
When God shall take the judgment throne,
   In Christ as Judge appearing.

Chapter 3

LIFE IMPARTED

I am come that they might have life, and that they might have it more abundantly.—JOHN 10:10.

We continue the record of the conversation with the man in the Inquiry Room.

"The first thing in salvation must be to get deliverance from the curse of the law.

"You can have *no peace* while uncertain as to your standing before God's law, in relation to the condemnation you know to be justly your due. If there is the shadow of the curse hanging over you, you cannot pray to God with any sense of acceptance or with any faith. You cannot really love God while expecting His wrath; and you cannot serve God acceptably until you love Him. On the other hand, God cannot bestow His Spirit upon you while you are under the curse of His law. So that of necessity FORGIVENESS OF SIN must be the *commencement* of the Christian life. And this comes, and is synonymous in the Gospel, with deliverance from the curse. Now, as nothing that you can do can take away the curse, it is something that God has to do for you. And if He does it for you, your part is to accept what He has done. Do you see the two points—Salvation before service: and, that as you cannot save yourself, God must save you?"

"I think I do. But how am I to accept of salvation?"

"By trusting Jesus Christ as your Savior. This I want you to do by trusting His Word. Will you now please read Galatians 3:13, the first part of the verse; and with it you may read the 14TH verse."

The man read:—

"Christ hath redeemed us from the curse of the law, being made a curse for us; that the blessing of Abraham might come on the Gentiles through Jesus Christ; that we might receive the promise of the Spirit through faith."

"Now, my friend, as you think of yourself as a sinner, and think of Christ's dying for you, and think of Him as loving you, with power and willingness to fully save you, are you, so far as you know your own heart, willing to surrender to Him, and accept Him as your Savior and your Lord?"

"Yes, I am."

"Well, thank God for that. Now, if accepting Christ means anything, it must mean that you will trust Him; and your trust will be manifested in believing His words. Do you believe the statement made in Galatians 3:13? Read it again, please."

"Christ hath redeemed us from the curse of the law, being made a curse for us."

"Do you believe it?" "Yes, I do."

"Are you redeemed?" "No, I am not."

"You are really willing to be saved, and are not consciously holding on to any sin you are unwilling to give up, and are willing to be Christ's, and accept Him?"

"Yes, I believe I am."

"Well then, once more: does not accepting Christ mean you will believe what He says? Please read this in 1 John 5:10."

"'He that believeth not God hath made Him a liar; because he believeth not the record that God gave of His Son.'"

"You see from this that God is trusted by trusting His Word; and that He is doubted by doubting His Word. Now will you believe in Christ, and take His word in Galatians 3:13 as true for you?"

"I will!"

"Very well. Are you redeemed?"

"No, I really cannot say that I am. I do not feel that I am."

"But, my friend, do you not see that the reason you do not feel that you are, is that you really have not yet believed God's Word? You do not look at *the Word* when I ask you if you are redeemed, but you look down into your *feelings*. Now God says that our hearts are 'deceitful above all things;' and your deceitful heart is never going to tell you that your sins are forgiven. And if it did tell you so you could not rely upon it. God tells us through His Word, not through our feelings, of our forgiveness, redemption, and salvation, on the ground of what Christ has done for us; and we accept it by believing His Word against our feelings. When we believe, there will be the result of believing, as in 1 John 5:10—

"'He that believeth on the Son of God hath the witness in himself.'"

"The believing comes first: and a man does not believe on the Son of God until, without feeling, he trusts His Word, because it is His Word, and not because he feels it. This trusting is the act of faith which unites the soul to Christ, and will indeed be followed by the witness, but never preceded. You are shut right up, as every soul is that comes to God, to that act of faith without feeling. So you see here in Ephesians 1:13—

"'After that ye believed, ye were sealed with that Holy Spirit of promise,' etc.

"The Spirit of God bears witness to us—first, as to our full salvation in Christ through the written Word. We must believe His witness there before He can do anything further for us. And it is as we believe it, and continue believing it, that He bears witness through it from God's Spirit to our spirit, that we are God's sons. This you will see is the meaning of Hebrews 10:15–18. The Spirit is there plainly spoken of as bearing witness through the Word. Now, to show you that your difficulty is—that you are not looking entirely away from self, and simply trusting the Word of God without reference to feeling, I will give you a little illustration to help you comprehend what it is to just trust God's bare Word.

"'CHRIST HATH REDEEMED!' Oh, joyful word,
    Let praise to God awaken,
On Christ the wrath of God outpoured,
    The curse from us hath taken.

"'CHRIST HATH REDEEMED!' The curse is gone,
    The Lord alone hath done it:
The Cross behold, with God's dear Son,
    And all our sins, upon it!

"'CHRIST HATH REDEEMED!' The law is met,

Its every claim exacted,
And God in justice now can meet
The soul in Christ perfected.

" 'CHRIST HATH REDEEMED!' The Word believe:
And Christ as Lord confessing,
Eternal life thou shalt receive,
And everlasting blessing."

Chapter 4

LIFE IMPARTED BY BELIEVING—ILLUSTRATION

He that believeth on the Son hath everlasting life.—JOHN 3:36.

The conversation in the Inquiry Room is still being continued.

"You know the Governor of this State has power, without accountability, to pardon any one he pleases, and to take them out of prison?"

"Yes, I do; and I know he sometimes pardons those he had better have left in. They come out, and are as big rogues as ever."

"No doubt. He cannot read men's hearts to tell whether they are truly repentant or not; but is liable to be deceived by their professions and the recommendations of their friends. God cannot be thus deceived; although men in folly and blindness seem to act as though they thought He might. And He, blessed be His name, gives with His pardon what the Governor has not power to give—grace in the heart to live the new and better life. But, to go on. We will suppose that the Governor sends down to the prison tomorrow pardons for three different men who are now there under sentence of ten, fifteen, or twenty years each of imprisonment for violation of law. The pardons are unconditional, are signed by the governor, and with them each of the men is at liberty to at once go out from the prison. But all three of the men have the notion firmly in their minds that there is something they must do before they can use the pardons that have been placed at their disposal. All of them take special pains with the petitions they think should be offered to the Governor on their behalf. And one waits until he has drawn up his petition, and had his friends numerously sign it; and armed with this and his pardon goes out of prison. Does the petition have anything to do with his getting out?"

"No, of course not. His pardon got him out."

"Well, the application of this is—the Lord does not want *you* to be occupied with praying and getting up petitions to Him to pardon you, while in His Word you may read the pardon, ready for your acceptance, to be taken by believing. The next of the prisoners is quite sure that he ought to feel very bad about his wrong-doing, and be able to weep over it, before it would be possible for him to use his pardon; and so he shuts himself up in his cell for a week, and works up this bad feeling, and then with swollen eyes presents his pardon and goes out. Have the swollen eyes anything to do with his release?"

"No; the pardon was all that was needed."

"So, my friend, your ideas about Repentance are all wrong, in so far as you regard repentance as a state of feeling bad, and think that God will be pleased with you when He sees you are feeling really bad; and that then because He is pleased with you, and you have satisfied His requirements in repenting enough, you are now worthy of the pardon. Repentance, in the Gospel sense of the word, is being honestly willing to yield to God, and accept His authority. It is produced by the view the Gospel gives of God's love in Christ, and the offer of His free pardon; and is evidenced as genuine by our willingness in yielding to God, to accept of that pardon and give him praise and thanks for the same, and *not* by our unbelieving neglect of the pardon, and being occupied with the vain thought of making ourselves worthy in God's sight by our feelings or our tears. Well, we come to the third prisoner. He also feels that he must do something before he takes the pardon, and so he obtains paper and ink, and writes out with much elaboration, style, and flourishing, a series of good resolutions showing what right ideas he has of generosity and good conduct, and in what a noble, upright manner the remainder of his life shall be passed. He signs his name at the bottom of the page, and holding up the paper for inspection, he is struck with admiration at the evidence of his own innate goodness; and now thinks that the Governor did quite the proper thing in pardoning him, and is sure that he has come into the proper frame to use the pardon, and that, accompanied by his good resolutions, it will get him out. Is he right?"

"No, of course not. The pardon did the business."

"Yes, my friend, it did; and God's pardon will do the business for you, if you will trust it. Good resolutions without the grace of God in our hearts to enable us to keep them are worse than useless. When Christ is accepted in the heart, new desires, new principles, and a new life will follow. But the first thing is—as a guilty, helpless, condemned sinner—to accept Christ; and not be wasting time in trying to make yourself better *before* you accept Him; or in making promises as to what you will do after you accept Him, with the idea that you earn your pardon in so doing.

"Let us follow the illustration a little further, to help you upon one remaining point—viz., your looking at your feelings. The three men are out of prison with their pardons in their pockets, and on their way to their homes. One of them is a man of morbid and unhappy temperament. A feeling of depression easily overcomes him. He is feeling bad as he goes on his way now. An officer meets and recognizes him, and says, 'See here. I know you. You were condemned by the law, and belong to the prison. What have you to show that you have a right to be out here?' The man hangs his head, and says, 'You are right. I belong to the prison. I will go back with you. I expected to feel very happy when I got out, but the feeling has not come; and, of course, I have no right to be out, feeling as I do. So I feel that I had better go back with you, and wait until I feel better.'"

"What is the matter with the man?"

"Why, the foolish fellow is talking about his feelings, instead of producing his pardon."

"Yes, just so. Well, here is the second one. He is an entirely different character, a happy, joyful, excitable temperament. He goes along whistling, singing, laughing, and telling everybody how happy he is. An officer meets him and recognizes him, and says, 'See here, friend, you were condemned, and belong by law to the prison. What have you to show for being out here?' 'Show,' says the man, 'why, don't you see how happy I feel? I know that a man that feels as happy as I feel must have a right to be out here. That's what I feel. I have my feelings to show.' But the officer collars him, and takes him off. What is the trouble?"

"Why, he is just as great a fool as the other man. He talks about his feelings instead of pulling out the pardon."

"Just so. Now a word about the third man; and I will make my application. He has determined in getting out of prison to live a new life. He is going to cut his bad companions, earn his bread, and live in a respectable way. He goes to a hairdresser, and buys a wig to hide his short hair. He goes to a tailor, and is nicely clothed. But the officer meets him and commands a halt, and says, 'See here, my man, I know you; you belong to the prison. You cannot fool me by your disguise. What have you to show for being out?' The man draws himself up with the dignity of injured innocence, and answers, 'Show, sir! I have my new and respectable character to show. I have turned over a new leaf. I am a reformed man. Do you see these new clothes? Do you see this wig? These are what I have to show, sir.' Before he has finished his speech the officer is hurrying him off to prison. What is the matter with this man?"

"Matter! Why, he is as great a fool as the other two: he does not pull out his pardon."

"Just so. Now, my friend, let us make the application. You say here tonight that, accepting your condemnation by God's law for your sins, as inevitable and just, you desire and are willing to accept Jesus Christ as your Redeemer, and from tonight trust His Word, and pray to Him as your Savior."

"Yes, sir, I am."

"Will you read once more Galatians 3:13?"

"Christ hath redeemed us from the curse of the law, being made a curse for us."

"Do you believe that?"

"Yes, I do."

"Are you redeemed?"

"Well, I—I don't feel ——"

"Stop! What did you say about those men who talked about their feelings, instead of holding up the Governor's pardon?"

"Oh, I see. Why, yes; that is it, is it not? Why, I haven't really believed it, have I? I am to trust God's Word to me, as those prisoners trusted the Governor's word to them; and feeling has nothing to do with it. How singular it is I did not see that before! Why, of course Christ has done it all. And I just accept it."

"Well, are you redeemed?"

"Yes, thank God, *I am*."

"How do you know you are?"

"Why, as a sinner I accept Jesus Christ as my Savior: and God's Word says I am redeemed; and I believe it."

"Well, my friend, praise God for the light that has come by believing. Look in the same direction for more to follow. And now, before we thank God, just see where your living for God comes in. Redeemed means purchased. What did Christ pay for you?"

"He paid His own life—His blood."

"Yes, dear friend, He did. Well, if He purchased you, and paid that price for you, to whom do you belong?"

"I belong to Him."

"Are you willing to have it so?—to be His property, His willing servant, His faithful follower, His obedient child?"

"I am. I belong to Christ. He redeemed me."

"Very well. That is the Christian life. It commences with redemption. We serve because we are saved. The curse is gone— *all* gone; and for ever gone. And now—with the Savior who died for us living to hear our prayer and provide a daily salvation from the power of sin—we are to live for our Redeemer.

"Let us praise Him!"

I Yield Myself to Jesus Christ

(Romans 6)

I yield myself to Jesus Christ,
    The Son of God, my Master;
He paid for me the ransom price,
    And saved me from disaster.

I once a servant was to sin,
    And to it wholly yielded;
The God of this world welcomed in,

His sceptre o'er me wielded.

But God the uncreated light
   In Jesus manifested,
Shone in upon my darkened night,
   And then I sin detested.

I strove in vain to break the chain
   By which my sins had bound me;
No strength had I to fight or fly,
   A lost one Jesus found me.

I saw myself nailed to the cross,
   In Him who thus was given,
To free me from the law's dread curse,
   And make me heir of Heaven.

And now by Him to law made dead,
   By faith I live united
To Him, my Lord, and risen Head,
   In holy union plighted.

Chapter 5

WARFARE

Fight the good fight of faith.—1 TIMOTHY 6:12.

fter ye were illuminated ye endured a great fight of afflictions," says the Word of God in Hebrews 10:32. LIFE involves warfare. Life is made manifest *in* warfare, and is developed and strengthened *by* warfare. This is the law of God in nature, and the law of God in grace. So, my brother, the trumpet of the Gospel gives no uncertain sound. We are called to WARFARE. In the spiritual world as in the natural, foes are permitted to exist: that we, as God's children, in fighting and overcoming them may grow in grace and strength, and make manifest the beauty and the power of that life which has been imparted to us to the praise and glory of our God. Therefore:

JAMES 1:2, 3—*Count it all joy when ye fall into divers temptations; knowing this, that the trying of your faith worketh patience.*

1 PETER 4:12, 13—*Beloved, think it not strange concerning the fiery trial which is to try you, as though some strange thing happened unto you: but rejoice, inasmuch as ye are partakers of Christ's*

sufferings; that when His glory shall be revealed, ye may be glad also with exceeding joy.

JOHN 15:2—*Every branch in Me that beareth fruit, He purgeth it, that it may bring forth more fruit.*

HEBREWS 12:6—*Whom the Lord loveth He chasteneth, and scourgeth every son whom He receiveth.*

1 PETER 5:10—*The God of all grace, who hath called us unto His eternal glory by Christ Jesus, after that ye have suffered awhile, make you perfect, stablish, strengthen, settle you.*

Thus the Lord puts before us our calling. The Lord is "the Lord of Hosts." "The Lord is a Man of War." All who follow Him are called unto conflict.

MATTHEW 16:24—*If any man will come after Me, let him deny himself, and take up his cross and follow Me.*

Let us ever bear in mind that this warfare comes "*after* we are illuminated"—comes because we are God's children, not to make us God's children. We are *working out* the salvation we have received, making manifest the life that God has put within us: working "with fear and trembling" indeed, in view of our terrible foes, and our constant need of divine help; and in view of the fact that "it is God which worketh in us, both to will and to do of His good pleasure."[1] But we are working not *for*, but *from* salvation. Illuminated, we stand as lights in this dark earth to shine for the glory of God, way-marks against which the world will rage—just as the waves of the ocean foam and toss themselves against the beacons on the coast, that have invaded their

---

1 Philippians 2:13.

domain to save the mariner from the ruin they would inflict.

God-hating devils and men have always hated God's children, and always will. A man wearing the English uniform, and bearing the English flag, passing through Upper Egypt today, would be an object of hate and persecution, and be in danger of death. He would be identified with a Government against which the people were fighting, and whose rule they refused. He would be in an enemy's territory, and could not have peace, if loyal to his country and to his flag. He *must* fight or throw off his uniform, and hide his colors. So a Christian in the world is in an enemy's country. God's rule is rebelled against; His authority despised; His very existence denied. We cannot be loyal to God on this earth without warfare—uncompromising, unceasing hostility to the very end. It is to this God calls us as His witnesses. If "illuminated," here is where we must stand—shoulder to shoulder with those who have girdled the earth with the name of Jesus; holding forth the Word of Life, standing fast for God and His truth: or basely hide our illumination, lay off our uniform, forsake our colors, and be at peace—false peace—with the enemies of our God. May God save us from this! "For whosoever shall be ashamed of Me and of My words, of him shall the Son of Man be ashamed when He shall come in His own glory, and in His Father's, and of the holy angels." (Luke 9:26.)

If discouraged or depressed in mind in view of the conflict, let us look up to Jesus, as commanded in Hebrews 12:2. Look to Jesus, the Princely Leader of our faith, who has gone on before us, enduring the cross, despising the shame. Let us remember the great cloud of witnesses: the saints and heroes who, upon earth's battlefield, have witnessed a good confession and died in the faith.

> "Once they were mourners here below
> And poured out cries and tears;

They wrestled hard as we do now,
   With sins, and doubts, and fears."

Let us go forth unto Christ in separation and communion, joining the host of sanctified ones who have suffered reproach for His name's sake; seeking here no continuing city, but looking for one to come: and then we shall be enabled, with a clear eye and a steady heart, to "run with patience the race that is set before us," and to fight on in the good fight of faith; and "having done all, to stand."

It is grand to be a soldier of Jesus Christ; for His soldiers are not for show, but for war.

FORWARD!

Forward then, with Jesus sharing
   In the warfare here below!
Forward! in His name unfearing,
   Boldly meeting every foe.

Count it never a disaster,
   When the shame for Him you bear,
But rejoice that such a Master,
   Gives you in His Cross a share.

Unto sin be daily dying,
   That His life may through thee shine;
Find thy strength in lowly lying
   At the pierced feet divine.

Soon the earthly conflict over,
   Christ will come to claim His own;
Oh, the grace—the grace, my brother!—
   If He then shall say "Well done!"

—D. W. WHITTLE

Chapter 6

OUR ENEMIES—SATAN

Your adversary, the devil, as a roaring lion, walketh about, seeking whom he may devour.—I Peter 5:8.

In warfare, to be forewarned is to be forearmed. God has given us abundance of forewarning, and knowledge of our adversaries, throughout His Word. Satan, the World, and the Flesh, are the three mighty foes of the child of God. The first is the mightiest; and is, indeed, the impelling and destroying element in the other two. To *him* we are specially pointed as the source of danger; and *of him* we are repeatedly warned. The child of God, subject to the Word of God, is made fully aware of the personality, the name, the history, the character, the plans and purposes, the power and final destiny, of this archfiend.

"I don't believe, Mr. Finney," said a man reckoned wise by the world to the faithful servant of Christ, "I don't believe in the existence of the devil."

"Don't you?" said the old man. "Well, my friend, you resist him for awhile, and you will believe in it."

So man, led captive by him at his will, either denies his existence or clothes him with hoofs and horns, a creature to be dreaded and shrunk from; instead of remembering the warning that he is *an angel of light*, presenting to each a tempting bait, and luring on in pleasant paths the soul to hell. Let the reader remember that never will he be in so great danger from Satan, as when careless and unconcerned as to his existence, and even questioning his personality.

The literal translation of the Lord's Prayer in the Revised Version, changing the words "Deliver us from *Evil*" to a faithful rendering of what our Lord taught, "Deliver us from the Evil *One*,"[1] has aroused enmity among unbelieving ones, who deny the supernatural. But let all who call Jesus Lord, remember that He taught us when we pray to say, "Deliver us from the Evil One."

Without examination of the passages where Satan is spoken of as a person under the name of "Evil Spirit" or "Wicked Spirit," and other designations, a glance at the Concordance will show that he is definitely mentioned as *a person* called "Satan," sixteen times in the Old Testament, and thirty-five times in the New. He is called "Devil" four times in the Old Testament, and one hundred and nine times in the New. He is called "Serpent" five times in the Old, and five times in the New Testament. He is one hundred and seventy-four times mentioned under these three designations. To say that no such person exists, or that his designation is simply a name for an evil influence or principle— is to make the Bible an untrustworthy book; the words of Jesus ambiguous and misleading; the history of man's redemption contradictory and falsifying, with its plans and purposes, and ultimate results and consequences, entirely changed from that which God has revealed in His Word. The existence of Satan as the enemy of God and prince of the powers of darkness can alone explain the existence of sin and the reign of misery and

1 Matthew 6:13.

death on this earth—can alone explain the coming of a Divine Redeemer to save man from his power, and the world from his awful reign.

Of his history before the creation of man, Jesus tells us in Luke 10:18, "I beheld Satan as lightning fall from heaven." And in 2 Peter 2:4, we read, "God spared not the angels that sinned, but cast them down to hell," etc. A few other intimations to the same effect are found in Job 1, Isaiah 14:12–15, Daniel 10:13, Zechariah 3:1, 2, and in Revelation; but nothing in detail beyond the words of Christ. *Our* concern is with his history on this earth, and our connection with that history. In regard to this the Word is plain and full. He appears in Genesis 3 as the denier of God's Word, "the liar from the beginning," the tempter, and the active agent in man's first transgression against God.

Declared to man as the cause of his fall and as his determined enemy, the history of his long relentless and most bitter warfare against the human race is briefly outlined in the words, "I will put enmity between thee and the woman, and between thy seed and her seed; it shall bruise thy head, and thou shalt bruise his heel," spoken by God to Satan in Genesis 3:15. The Bible, from *that* verse to Revelation 20:10, where "the devil that deceived them is cast into the lake of fire and brimstone, to be tormented day and night for ever and ever," is a history of that warfare. Read in the light of this prophecy, it becomes intelligible and most deeply interesting. The conflict at once commences, and proceeds with deepening interest and intensity down to the end, when Satan is cast out, and the Son of God, in the form of the Son of Man, with His elect "redeemed of Adam's race," in bodies like His own, reign over earth, an Eden once again—the paradise of Christ the Bridegroom, and the Church His Bride—where sin can never enter.

Cain is possessed of Satan, and as a consequence Abel is

murdered. This was the devil's first success.

God's children mix with the seed of Cain, and soon become corrupt, and in judgment are swept away by the flood. This was the devil's second triumph.

Noah delivered from the flood is overcome by wine. His children multiplied; are far from God at Babel, and under Satan's power. They are scattered over the earth, and left to follow the inclinations of their own deceitful hearts; while God, to make a people for His name out from the sons of Adam, and *fulfil the promise* of the woman's seed, calls Abram.

From that call in Genesis 12, the Word of God is the history of Satan's warfare against *Abram and his seed*. He hindered the birth of Isaac; he strove to have him killed; he made enmity between Esau and Jacob; and he sought the death of Joseph, for fear that *he* would be the one to bruise his head. When God revealed that the promised seed should come through *Judah,* then against *Judah* and *his line*, is Satan's malice shown. With this in view, how things recorded that seem strange within God's holy book are all explained! The vilest sins the Bible records are sins recorded of those who were in the *chosen line*. And these sins they were tempted by Satan to commit, to bring them under judgment, and to thwart God's purposes and plans. But, with each sin the gospel is foreshadowed by *redemption* acted out in type; and the seed is preserved.

No nation ever sinned so grievously, or came so many times so near destruction, as Israel. The devil thought he had them all when under Pharaoh down in Egypt. They lived in sin, and wrought in bondage. But God raised up a little babe, and had him nursed in Pharaoh's house; and by that babe, a man of stammering lips, He delivered them. At Sinai, Satan brought them all right under judgment in leading them to vow they would keep God's law, and then in ten days after they bowed, and worshipped *him* before the golden calf. The sword of God was drawn above the dancing, naked, guilty host; but *one man's* pleading of the promises of God beside the blood-stained altar—a type of Christ for us in heaven—defeated Satan; and the seed was spared.

When out of Judah's tribe the *house of David* was chosen, a thousand years before the birth of Christ, as being in the royal line through which the promised seed should come, then Satan fought with *them*. Many of the Psalms of David tell the conflict he endured; a conflict typical of that to be endured by *Christ* and *by His Church*. The sin of David was Satan's work. The murder of his sons, the fall of Solomon, the cutting off of the seed royal, until only one young babe was left—miraculously preserved (2 Chronicles 22:11); the carrying into Babylon, the princes there among the lions, and in the fiery furnace—all show how desperately Satan fought against *the woman's seed*.

In the fullness of time, from *David's family* and from *Judah's tribe*, of *Abraham's seed*, Jesus Christ our Lord was born. With His appearance on the earth, the warfare centers upon *Him*. His life is sought while yet a babe; and from the commencement to the close of His ministry the devil fought as never before. In Matthew 4 we have the conflict of temptation in the wilderness, when the tempter appeared as A PERSON, called the *devil,* and is addressed by Christ as *Satan*. Thrust through and through by the Word of God, the sword of the Spirit, and defeated in this attempt to turn aside the "Second Adam" from His trust in God, he leaves Him "for *a season*" (Luke 4:13); but soon renews the fight, through Priests and Pharisees, Herods and Pilates, and wicked men, with whom the powers of hell were leagued. He withstood Christ at every step of His pathway by entering into the Jews who opposed and denied Him, of whom He said, "Ye are of your father the devil; and the lusts of your father ye will do." "Now ye seek to kill Me" (John 8:44, 40). He entered into

Judas, who betrayed the Lord.

He was present in the Garden of Gethsemane, not to *sleep,* as did the faithful disciples; but to actively torment, with every temptation that hellish ingenuity could contrive, the Man of Sorrows, as He lonely wrestled there in prayer, with wicked spirits all around, until there came the overcoming grace. In the darkness of the Cross Satan was present, and "bruised the heel" of the promised seed. "'Twas all that he could do." Beyond God's Word, he has *never* gone, and *never can go*—that Word now waits to be fulfilled *on him.*

In the meantime, O Christian believer, what means this record—this minute and awful delineation of Satan's triumphs over man—for you? Are *we,* as those who in our little time upon this earth, are now the special objects of his wrath, standing in the forefront of a conflict raging hotter every generation as the end draws near—awake to our danger; and alive to the dignity of our calling as sharers with Christ in His sufferings, and heirs of coming glory? May the eyes of the reader be opened to the reality of the spiritual conflict that has been raging on this earth since Adam's fall, and to the part he or she must individually have in that conflict, as bearing the name of Christ.

EPHESIANS 6:12, R. V.—*For our wrestling is not against flesh and blood, but against the principalities, against the powers, against the world-rulers of this darkness, against the spiritual hosts of wickedness in the heavenlies.*

Chapter 7

OUR ENEMIES—SATAN *(continued)*

The dragon, that old serpent, which is the Devil and Satan.
—REVELATION 20:2.

From the testimony brought forward in the preceding chapter, the reality of Satan's warfare against *Israel* and against *Christ* would be admitted by all who bow to the authority of God's Word. It is, however, when we come to study Satan's relations to *the Church* that we find Scripture testimony in much larger quantity, and more direct and simple, if possible, in character: teaching that—all through her history on this earth, right down to the Resurrection morning, when, with the glorious appearing of the Lord, Satan will be bound—the Church, and each individual in the Church, must fight the Devil, and will often suffer from him as a most malignant foe. The experience of Job is undoubtedly given to teach the Christian this, with the caution, that we are not to look for an end, like Job's, this side of Resurrection.

Plagued more than those that are around us, the trial to faith is great, and it is only the faith that grasps the resurrection hope, and can say, with Job, "I *know* that my Redeemer liveth, and that He shall stand at the latter day upon the earth: and though, after my skin, worms destroy this body, yet in my flesh shall I see God,"[1] that will stand the trial.

David, in the experience related in the seventy-third Psalm, had almost fainted under it. His "feet had well nigh slipped." The wicked prospered, and were at ease, while God's people were chastened and oppressed. He sang, "When I thought to know this, it was too painful for me." The burden was heavy upon him; for he had to pass through bitter trials. And to how many of God's dear children since has this been their most painful trial! Dear reader, enter with David into the sanctuary of God.

See from His Word in the record of Job and David, and, above all, from the example of our blessed Lord, that the trials through which you are now passing have the same origin as theirs; and the same faithful God who brought all to a happy issue with them, will, as you trust Him, bring all to a happy issue with you. Judge not of things on earth according to man's judgment; but consider the *latter end* of all things here, and judge as in the sunlight of God's eternal throne.

There was scriptural authority and true wisdom in the answer given by a Christian negro slave to his master in the South, when one day, after his master had overheard him groaning and weeping and praying to God for deliverance from the Devil, and had said to him, "Pompey, you seem to have a good deal of trouble with the Devil; and he does not trouble me a bit. Yet you are a good praying man; and I am not a Christian at all. How does that come about, Pompey?" He replied: "Ah, Massa, I will soon explain that. When you are out shooting ducks, which do you send the dog after first, Massa, the ones that fall dead, or the ones that are wounded a little, and are trying to get away?" "Why, Pompey, the wounded ones, of course. The dead ones we

1 Job 19:25, 26.

are sure of, and can take our time to pick them up." "Just so, Massa. And so it is with Satan. He has got all of those that are not born again, fast and sure. But those that *know the Lord*, and that are *getting away*, He sets all his dogs after; while he picks up the others by and by." A solemn answer for Pompey's master, and for all who are like him, without Christ, unconcerned for sin, and untroubled in a world where Satan reigns.

"And the Lord said, Simon, Simon, Satan hath desired to have you that he may sift you as wheat. But I have prayed for thee, that thy faith fail not" (Luke 22:31, 32). And Satan was permitted to have Peter—not to enter and possess him, as he did Judas, who never was a child of God, but—to have him in the sense of being let loose upon him, to tempt him and to overcome him, for the humbling of Peter's pride and for sifting out his self-confidence, God overruling all that Satan did for Peter's spiritual good and His own glory. Now, Peter's experience is a type of the experience of the whole Church and of the individuals of the Church. In each generation of its history the Church has been sifted by Satan. He changes from age to age the agencies employed; but his malice is unchanged, and the results are still the same. Persecution at one period: prosperity at another. Truth without the Holy Spirit in one age: false doctrine following. Contempt from the world, in this generation: world-conformity, in the next. Zeal without knowledge, breaking out into fanaticism, and dividing the Church: knowledge without zeal, ending in materialism, and paralyzing the Church. Ecclesiasticism and spiritual oppression, dwarfing the Church: lawless liberty, with no recognition of scriptural authority, scattering the Church.

And so the body of Christ has been, and is being, sifted; and will continue to be sifted unto the end. What the Holy Ghost has recorded of its early history, He has prophesied should be its experience until Satan should be bound.

But let the Word speak for itself upon this deeply important subject. May the reader attentively ponder its solemn testimony, as we glance along its pages from the days of Pentecost *down to the close.*

ACTS 5:3—*Ananias, why hath Satan filled thine heart to lie to the Holy Ghost?*

ACTS 13:10—*Child of the Devil, enemy of all righteousness, wilt thou not cease to pervert the right ways of the Lord?*

ACTS 26:17, 18—*Delivering thee from the Gentiles, unto whom now I send thee, to open their eyes, and to turn them from darkness to light, and from the power of Satan unto God, that they may receive forgiveness of sins, and inheritance among them which are sanctified by faith that is in Me.*

ROMANS 16:20—*The God of peace shall bruise Satan under your feet shortly.*

1 CORINTHIANS 5:5—*To deliver such an one unto Satan for the destruction of the flesh.*

1 CORINTHIANS 7:5—*That Satan tempt you not.*

2 CORINTHIANS 2:11—*Lest Satan should get an advantage of us: for we are not ignorant of his devices.*

2 CORINTHIANS 11:3—*But I fear, lest by any means, as the serpent beguiled Eve through his subtilty, so your minds should be corrupted from the simplicity that is in Christ.*

2 CORINTHIANS 11:14, 15—*Satan himself is transformed into an angel of light. Therefore it is no great thing if his ministers also be transformed as the ministers of righteousness; whose end shall be according to their works.*

2 CORINTHIANS 12:7—*And lest I should be exalted above measure through the abundance of the revelations, there was given to me a thorn in the flesh, the messenger of Satan to buffet me, lest I should be exalted above measure.*

EPHESIANS 2:2—*Wherein in time past ye walked according to the course of this world, according to the prince of the power of the air, the spirit that now worketh in the children of disobedience.*

EPHESIANS 6:11—*Put on the whole armour of God, that ye may be able to stand against the wiles of the devil.*

1 THESSALONIANS 2:18—*Wherefore we would have come unto you, even I Paul, once and again; but Satan hindered us.*

2 THESSALONIANS 2:8–10—*And then shall that Wicked be revealed, whom the Lord shall consume with the spirit of His mouth, and shall destroy with the brightness of His coming: even Him, whose coming is after the working of Satan; with all power, and signs, and lying wonders; and with all deceivableness of unrighteousness in them that perish, because they received not the love of the truth, that they might be saved.*

1 TIMOTHY 3:7—*The snare of the devil.*

1 TIMOTHY 4:1—*Now the Spirit speaketh expressly, that in the latter times some shall depart from the faith, giving heed to seducing spirits, and doctrines of devils.*

1 TIMOTHY 5:15—*For some are already turned aside after Satan.*

2 TIMOTHY 2:26, 3:1—*That they may recover themselves out of the snare of the devil, who are taken captive by him at his will. This know also, that in the last days perilous times shall come.* (May I urge upon the reader to turn to and carefully read the whole of this chapter.)

HEBREWS 2:14, 15—*Forasmuch then as the children are par-takers of flesh and blood, He also himself likewise took part of the same; that through death He might destroy him that had the power of death—that is, the devil; and deliver them who through fear of death were all their lifetime subject to bondage.*

JAMES 4:7—*Resist the devil, and he will flee from you.*

1 PETER 5:8, 9 (R. V.)—*Be sober, be watchful: your adversary the devil, as a roaring lion, walketh about, seeking whom he may devour; whom withstand, stedfast in your faith, knowing that the same suf-ferings are accomplished in your brotherhood who are in the world.*

1 JOHN 2:13—*I write unto you, young men, because ye have overcome the Wicked One.*

1 JOHN 3:8, 10—*He that committeth sin is of the devil; for the devil sinneth from the beginning. For this purpose the Son of God was manifested, that He might destroy the works of the devil. In this the children of God are manifest, and the children of the devil: whosoever doeth not righteousness is not of God, neither he that loveth not his brother.*

1 JOHN 3:12—*Not as Cain, who was of that Wicked One, and slew his brother.*

1 JOHN 4:1–3—*Beloved, believe not every spirit; but try the spir-its whether they are of God. . . . Every spirit that confesseth that Jesus Christ is come in the flesh is of God. And every spirit that confesseth not that Jesus Christ is come in the flesh is not of God. And this is that spirit of Antichrist, whereof ye have heard that it should come: and even now already is it in the world.*

1 JOHN 5:18 TO 21 (R. V.)—*We know that whosoever is begotten of God sinneth not; but he that was begotten of God keepeth him, and*

the Evil One toucheth him not. We know that we are of God; and the whole world lieth in the Evil One. And we know that the Son of God is come, and hath given us an understanding that we may know Him that is true; and we are in Him that is true, even in His Son Jesus Christ. This is the true God, and eternal life. My little children, guard yourselves from idols.

2 JOHN 7 (R. V.)—*Many deceivers are gone forth into the world, even they that confess not that Jesus the Christ cometh in the flesh. This is the deceiver and the Antichrist.*

JUDE 9—*Yet Michael the Archangel, when contending with the devil he disputed about the body of Moses, durst not bring against him a railing accusation, but said, The Lord rebuke thee.*

REVELATION 2:10 (R. V.).—*To Smyrna—"Fear not the things which thou art about to suffer; behold, the devil is about to cast some of you into prison that ye may be tried; and ye shall have tribulation ten days. Be thou faithful unto death; and I will give thee a crown of life."*

REVELATION 2:20, 23, 25 (R. V.).—*To Thyatira—"I have this against thee, that thou sufferest the woman Jezebel, which calleth herself a prophetess; and she teacheth and seduceth my servants. . . . And I will kill her children with death. . . . But to you, I say, to the rest that are in Thyatira, as many as have not this teaching, which know not the deep things of Satan . . . Hold fast till I come."*

REVELATION 3:10, 11 (R. V.).—*To Philadelphia—"Because thou didst keep the word of my patience, I also will keep thee from the hour of trial, that hour which is to come upon the whole world to try them that dwell upon the earth. I come quickly: hold fast that which thou hast, that no one take thy crown."*

REVELATION 9:11—*And they had a king over them, which is*

the angel of the bottomless pit, whose name in the Hebrew tongue is Abaddon, but in the Greek tongue hath his name Apollyon (margin, destroyer).

REVELATION 12:7–13, 17—*And there was war in heaven: Michael and his angels fought against the dragon; and the dragon fought and his angels, and prevailed not; neither was their place found any more in heaven. And the great dragon was cast out, that old serpent, called the devil, and Satan, which deceiveth the whole world: he was cast out into the earth, and his angels were cast out with him. And I heard a loud voice saying in heaven, Now is come salvation, and strength, and the kingdom of our God, and the power of His Christ; for the accuser of our brethren is cast down, which accused them before our God day and night. And they overcame him by the blood of the Lamb, and by the word of their testimony: and they loved not their lives unto the death. Therefore rejoice, ye heavens, and ye that dwell in them. Woe to the inhabiters of the earth and of the sea! for the devil is come down unto you, having great wrath, because he knoweth that he hath but a short time. And when the dragon saw that he was cast unto the earth, he persecuted the woman which brought forth the man-child. . . . And the dragon was wroth with the woman, and went to make war with the remnant of her seed, which keep the commandments of God, and have the testimony of Jesus Christ.*

REVELATION 13:6–8 AND 15–17—*And he opened his mouth in blasphemy against God, to blaspheme His name, and His tabernacle, and them that dwell in heaven. And it was given unto him to make war with the saints, and to overcome them: and power was given him over all kindreds, and tongues, and nations. And all that dwell upon the earth shall worship him, whose names are not written in the book of life of the Lamb slain from the foundation of the world. . . . And he had power to give life unto the image of the beast, that the image of the beast should both speak, and cause that as many as would not*

worship the image of the beast should be killed. And he causeth all,
both small and great, rich and poor, free and bond, to receive a mark
in their right hand, or in their foreheads; and that no man might buy
or sell, save he that had the mark, or the name of the beast, or the
number of his name.

REVELATION 20:1 TO 10—*And I saw an angel come down from*
heaven, having the key of the bottomless pit and a great chain in his
hand. And he laid hold on the dragon, that old serpent, which is the
devil, and Satan, and bound him a thousand years, and cast him into
the bottomless pit, and shut him up, and set a seal upon him, that he
should deceive the nations no more, till the thousand years should be
fulfilled: and after that he must be loosed a little season. And I saw
thrones; and they sat upon them, and judgment was given unto them:
and I saw the souls of them that were beheaded for the witness of Jesus,
and for the Word of God, and which had not worshipped the beast,
neither his image, neither had received his mark upon their foreheads,
or in their hands; and they lived and reigned with Christ a thousand
years. But the rest of the dead lived not again until the thousand
years were finished. This is the first resurrection. Blessed and holy is
he that hath part in the first resurrection: on such the second death
hath no power; but they shall be priests of God and of Christ, and
shall reign with Him a thousand years. And when the thousand years
are expired, Satan shall be loosed out of his prison, and shall go out
to deceive the nations which are in the four quarters of the earth, Gog
and Magog, to gather them together to battle: the number of whom is
as the sand of the sea. And they went up on the breadth of the earth,
and compassed the camp of the saints about, and the beloved city: and
fire came down from God out of heaven, and devoured them. And the
devil that deceived them was cast into the lake of fire and brimstone,
where the beast and the false prophet are, and shall be tormented day
and night for ever and ever.

WOE, WOE TO EARTH!

Woe, woe to earth! The devil has come down,
    From heaven cast out. The earth is now his home;
And here he seeks in rage to rob Christ of His crown,
    And make the sons of Adam share his awful doom.

Once there in heaven, with access to God's throne,
    He day and night accused our fallen guilty race,
Insisting that God's justice should be justly shown,
    And man no longer left to live, his Maker to disgrace.

But when the Son of God as "Son of Man" had come,
    And on the cross, for guilty man, a full atonement made,
God pointed to His sprinkled blood before the Throne,
    And Satan from those heavenly courts in wrath for ever fled.

But, woe to earth!—and sorrow for a little while
    To Christ's believing ones who witness for Him here.
With malice and with rage, with traps and cunning guile,
    The doomed he lures to death; the saints he fights with fear.

He knows his time is short: that soon the Son of God
    Victorious shall come, and bind him with the everlasting chain:
And so he rages on, and fills the world with blood!
    And earth must groan till Christ shall come to reign.

Chapter 8

OUR ENEMIES—SATAN *(concluded)*

For we are not ignorant of his devices. —2 CORINTHIANS 2:11.

hus, in detail, has been given the testimony of the Holy Ghost concerning Satan and his relation to the Church and the individual Christian.

How can there be any intelligent comprehension of the character of Christian conflict on this earth, without an understanding of the rebellion against God and His righteous government that Satan has instigated and is leading on; and the knowledge that there are just two parties on the earth still, as at the beginning—viz., *the seed of the woman* and *the seed of the serpent*—and between them WAR. The Lord Jesus Christ has overcome Satan, and in His Word has exposed and unmasked him as a *murderer*, a *deceiver*, a *liar*, an *accuser*, a *blasphemer*, a *wicked one*, an *adversary*, a *seducer*, a *corrupter*, a *beguiler*, and a *roaring lion*. The Lord would have us know him as he really is, that we may fear and abhor him. He warns us that he will approach us as "an angel of light,"[1] and will assume the character most likely to secure his prey. Abiding in Christ, and in humility guided by His Word, we shall be kept by His power. If caught

1 2 Corinthians 11:14.

by Satan away from Christ, and puffed up by spiritual pride or wilfulness of the flesh, we shall assuredly be captured by him in some way. We must be ever upon our guard against the *first approaches* of the enemy, "avoiding every appearance of evil."[1]

Some years since a soldier was posted in a forest as a sentry, to watch for the approach of Indians. It was a position of peculiar danger. Savages were known to be lurking in the woods around the fort, watching for an opportunity to attack or to cut off the sentinels. Three different men had been surprised and killed without having had time to fire a shot, in three successive preceding days, upon this post. The soldier was left with strict orders for the utmost vigilance to be observed. Reflecting upon his situation, as he was left alone, the man determined that he would allow no living thing to approach him under any circumstances without having a satisfactory explanation of what it was. In a short time, an object moving among the trees at some distance caught his eye. He watched it attentively, with gun at the ready, until, as it came a little nearer, he saw it was a wild hog common to the country, and which soon disappeared. Another came in sight. It made less impression upon him. He satisfied himself it *was* a wild hog, rooting under the leaves, and eating the nuts that had fallen from the trees. Presently, off in another direction the leaves were rustled, and a third wild hog appeared. Being now used to these creatures, he gave but little attention; but with gun still ready, he watched for other objects. The movements of the last animal, however, soon again engaged the man's thoughts. It had been gradually approaching him while his attention had been withdrawn to other objects, and was now quite near. The minuteness with which he had observed the two first animals, to satisfy himself that they were *real* beasts, led him to observe a slight awkwardness in the movements of this

1 See 1 Thessalonians 5:22.

one. He saw that it was a possibility that an Indian might be covered by the skin of an animal, and thus be approaching him. If it *was* an Indian, the safest thing for him to do was to shoot. If it was not an Indian, but simply a hog, and he should shoot, his comrades would jeer at him. He wisely resolved that he would run no risk; and as the object continued its approach, he raised his rifle to his shoulder, took aim, and fired. With a bound and a yell, an Indian leaped to his feet, and fell back dead.

One man had saved his life, and probably prevented the surprise of the garrison, by his watchfulness, where others had lost their lives by their carelessness. So the child of God must be ever on the alert, and guarded against the approaches of the Evil One. Draw the Word of God upon *every object* that approaches you in this dark world of sin. If the devil is in it, you may be sure the Word will expose him. Stripped of his disguise, he will jump up and howl, and will leave you. He has been once defeated by the Lord Jesus *with the Word*. He has never recovered from the defeat, and never will. In the name of Christ, *with the same Word*, we can ever have the victory. Without Christ, and in our own strength or wisdom, we shall suffer defeat.

As examples of the use of the Word in overcoming the tempter, a friend of the writer, an Irishman, has told him how, shortly after his conversion, one night, on his return from a meeting where he had been speaking and dealing with inquirers up to a late hour, as he lay upon the lounge in his sitting-room for a few moments' rest, it seemed as though a voice spoke in his soul, "You have been preaching tonight about the *joy* of being a Christian. Where is your joy? You know you do not feel a bit of joy. You have not a bit of feeling of love now in your heart to Christ. You are a hypocrite, and not saved at all. You had better just give this all up." It seemed very dark to him for a minute. It was all true, so far as his *feeling* was concerned. He was so mentally exhausted that a reaction had set in, and he *could not feel;* and if he had left the issue right there, Satan would have had the victory. But presently, he reached for his Bible, and opened to John 5:24, the verse that had been used to bring him to Christ, and read, "Verily, verily, I say unto you, he that heareth My Word, and believeth on Him that sent Me, hath everlasting life, and shall not come into condemnation, but is passed from death unto life." Then, thanking God that *the Word* had not gone, though his feelings had, he says, "I just held the Bible, with my finger on that verse, under the sofa, for I knew the devil always lurked in the darkest places, and told him to just look at that, and go away and leave me alone; and he did. I went to bed in peace."

So a dear servant of the Lord in Scotland much used of God was brought into the light as to the assurance of faith by cannily cross-questioning a man not long converted, whose happy testimony that Christ had saved him, he had heard. "But," said he to the man, "do you never have doubts troubling you, as to whether your sins are certainly forgiven?"

"Plenty of times," said the man, "the devil comes around whispering his doubts."

"Well, what do you do?"

"Do? Why, I have *no argument* with him. I just go right to God's Word, and tell him I believe what God says, and that I don't believe him. Why, man, I believe if we stop to *argue* with the devil, he would make us doubt our own existence."

Light broke in upon the mind of the inquirer as to the weapon to be used in meeting the adversary; and he has since had the victory by faith.

Martin Luther's views as to the personality and power of Satan, and the account of his spiritual wrestling with him, are well known. And there is nothing peculiar in Luther's experience.

Knox and the men of the Reformation all had the same. Ridley, Bunyan, Baxter, and the saints of their day, verily fought with real powers of darkness, and waxed valiant in the fight, made intense and earnest for God by the realization that the forces, working without them or within them, that opposed righteousness, were inspired by and in league with hell.

An eminent servant of God in our own day has repeatedly said, "I have an increasing fear of Satan, and feel an increasing need, as God is using me in His service, of keeping closer and closer to Him who alone can keep me from Satan's power. He ever aims to draw away and use to God's dishonor those who have been brought nearest to Christ. He went right among the twelve to find one to betray Him, and another to deny Him; and so when God is using us we should be doubly on our guard."

Billy Bray, the Cornish miner, whose rugged piety and real consistent consecration to Christ's service have been made a blessing to so many hundreds of God's children, gives much instruction, in his quaint way, as to how to treat the temptations of Satan. He says of himself that, one day, when he was a little down-hearted, he stood upon the brink of a coal-pit; and some one seemed to say, "Now, Billy, just throw yourself down there and be rid of all your trouble." He knew in a minute who it was, and, drawing back, said, "Oh no, Satan, you can just throw yourself down there. That is your way home; but I am going to my home in a different direction." Another time he tells us that his *crop of potatoes* turned out poorly; and as he was digging them in the fall, Satan was at his elbow, and said, "There, Billy, isn't that poor pay for serving your Father the way you have all the year? Just see those small potatoes." He stopped his hoeing, and replied, "Ah, Satan, at it again, talking against my Father; bless His name. Why, when I served you, I didn't get any potatoes at all. What are you talking against Father for?" And on he went hoeing and praising the Lord for small potatoes. A valuable lesson for us all.

Satan says of every child of God, as he did of old of Job, "Doth he serve God for nought?"[1] And we must have the testing of being brought to *small* potatoes that the reality of our faith may be shown, God vindicated, and Satan rebuked.

So, for the honor of our blessed God, and for the glory of our dear Redeemer, let us "resist the devil" in his attempts to poison our mind with false doctrines, *denying* God's Word; in his solicitations to the flesh to yield to that which would be *disobedient* to the Word; in his insidious efforts to lead us, as Christians, into world-conformity that would *compromise* the Word.

And let the young Christian remember, whence come the evil thoughts that often dart through the mind—sometimes even when he is engaged in the most holy exercises—and let him not be *unduly* cast down because of these evil suggestions. He who tempted our Lord is permitted to tempt us. We are not held as responsible for wicked thoughts, unless the evil thought is harbored and cherished in the breast, and the sinful suggestion welcomed and delighted in. As an old writer has said: "We cannot hinder the birds flying over us, and sometimes unawares lighting upon our heads; but we *can* hinder their building nests in our hair: and so, although we cannot hinder Satan suggesting the most awful, blaspheming, vile, and unbelieving thoughts to our minds, we *can* hinder their entrance into our hearts by the simple cry to Jesus, and the turning of the mind to Him." "Look unto Me, and be ye saved,"[2] is a precious promise to plead when thus assaulted. "Resist the devil" in the name of Jesus, and he *will* flee from you.[3]

---

1 See Job 1:9.

2 Isaiah 45:22.

3 See James 4:7.

Ever Watchful

Ever watchful, on thy guard,
　Child of God, thy way pursue;
Holding fast the gleaming sword,
　Where the hosts of hell may view.

Keep thy Leader e'er in sight,
　From His footsteps never stray;
Turn not to the left or right,
　Onward, upward, make thy way!

Though thy dearest friend entreat,
　Know that Satan's surely there,
If in sin, however sweet,
　Thou art asked to have a share.

Count that man thy direst foe,
　Though affection he profess,
If he seek to have thee go
　Where God's will thou must transgress.

Hate the devil, fear his power,
　For deliverance daily pray;
Trust in Christ from hour to hour,
　Make His promises thy stay.

Chapter 9

THE WORLD

Love not the world, neither the things that are in the world.
—I JOHN 2:15.

he attention has already been called to the testimony of God's Word that the devil is *the god* of this world, its *prince*, and its *ruler;* and that "the world lieth in the Evil One" (1 John 5:19, R. V.). This would be sufficient to indicate the imperative necessity of one chosen by the Lord Jesus Christ to be His child being separated from the world. He Himself has said, "They are not of the world, even as I am not of the world" (John 17:16). "If ye were of the world, the world would love his own; but because ye are not of the world, but I have chosen you out of the world, therefore the world hateth you" (John 15:19).

Now the "world" as here spoken of does not mean the *material earth* on which we live, with its mountains and hills, valleys and plains, oceans and lakes, rivers and brooks; with its trees, fruits, and flowers: these are all good, and created for man's good, in gratification of the physical senses to which they are adapted, and for which they were created. But it is a generic term, describing the *spirit* of those who, living in this world, live for *this alone*, and make the gratifications of their desires for *things here* the end of their being, with no recognition of God's claims upon them, and no care for their souls.

1 John 2:16 speaks of this *spirit of worldliness*, under the term of "the world," and describes what it means as being "the *lust of the flesh,* and the *lust of the eyes, and the pride of life.*" Now the vast majority of the people on this earth are living under the power of these three things; and they are said in Scripture to *"love the world,"* for this spirit is characteristic of the world. The Christian lives surrounded by this atmosphere. He is brought into contact with it upon every side. It controls the politics, the society, the literature, the amusements, and the popular religion of our age, as it has of every age since Christ was crucified. But, although surrounded by it, the Christian is to keep from *breathing it:* he is to live as one already in Heaven, looking down upon earth; his life, his joy, his citizenship, are up yonder. A man standing erect on the earth breathes air of a purer quality than that breathed by the insects that crawl at his feet; so the man risen with Christ should stand erect as a new man in Christ Jesus, and breathe the air of Heaven. Vital connection with Christ by faith, and the maintenance of that connection by believing prayer and communion through God's Word, alone enable him to do this. If believing fellowship with Christ is interrupted, the air of Heaven ceases to flow around him; he grovels in earthly things, and drinks in the atmosphere of this world. "If ye then be risen with Christ, seek those things which are above, where Christ sitteth on the right hand of God. Set your affection on things above, and not on things on the earth" (Colossians 3:1, 2).

This recognition of the *enmity of the world* is of the utmost importance to the young Christian. By *enmity,* it is not to be understood that the world will always persecute, and war in this way against the Christian. But it rather means that the distinctive spirit of the world, godlessness and selfishness, is antagonistic and opposed to the Spirit of God; so that whenever and wherever a child of God compromises in any way with the world, he is certain to receive injury thereby. This is the meaning of the words, "The friendship of the world is enmity with God: whosoever therefore will be a friend of the world is the enemy of God" (James 4:4). So that it is absolutely certain that if a man is wholly yielded to God, and has the purpose of pleasing God in his walk on the earth, he will be brought to separate himself from that which is distinctively and distinctly *of the world*. He will be *in* the world as the ship is *in* the sea; but the world is not to be *in* him, as the sea is not *in* the ship.

We are to make Jesus our example. He did not *withdraw* from the world, but mingled freely with all classes of men, going where He was invited; but ever taking advantage of the opportunities offered Him by thus mingling with the people, to teach them of God and do them good. His motive in all things was to *please the Father*. He could say truthfully, "I do *always* those things that please Him" (John 8:29). We are told that, "as the Father sent Him *into* the world, even so has He sent us *into* the world" (John 17:18).

We are not to withdraw from the world as recluses, but to mingle with our fellowmen, and seek in all ways to lead them Godward. We are to own the ties of family and the ties of country, and to have sympathy for all humanity, even as we have Him for our example. He, when on earth, was a familiar guest in the homes of the people. He took the little children up in His arms and blessed them. He was present at the marriage feast and in the house of mourning. He went regularly to the feasts at Jerusalem, and in all places and at all times was ever accessible to and in sympathy with man. But in doing this He ever retained His character as a heavenly Man.

In the home where He was the guest, whether it was the house of Martha, of Simon, or of Zacchaeus, *He led the conversation* and spoke of God. We cannot conceive that He ever occupied His precious time in talking with Martha and Mary about Herod's *last ball*, or the *theatrical entertainments* and *operatic performances* at the Jerusalem theatre, or gossiped with them about the latest Roman fashions or the last scandal at Herod's palace.

Nor would He be led by Simon and the Pharisees to spend the dinner-hour in discussing ecclesiastical politics and criticizing the latest speeches in the Sanhedrim. Nor by Zacchaeus, into a calculation as to the future course of the stock market and the movements in the commercial world.

Filled with love and benevolence, a citizen of Heaven, with a vision that swept eternity, He moved here below, a Man among men; but a heavenly-minded Man—never allowing Himself to be dragged down by men to a *worldly* level, but ever seeking to lift up the men of the world to the plain of heavenly things where He abode. Filled with the love to the Father, He made the most common actions of daily life beautiful and divine in character by the manifestation of a divine Spirit in their performance. He "pleased not Himself,"[1] but was separated from the world as far as Heaven is from earth, in the spirit of His mind, by the *motive* that ever governed Him—to please God His Father. With Him thus presented as our Example, how simple the path is made for us to tread as we go through this world! He *has* left us an example, indeed; and for the distinct purpose—"that we should follow His steps."

It is not of special use to present a series of specific rules, and to particularize as to the various things that a Christian is called to give up and separate from in giving up "the world." Rules might

1 Romans 15:3.

be prepared, and, indeed, have been, of the most ascetic character; and men and women have conformed to them, and yet have
utterly failed in the *spirit of their minds* in giving up the world.

The Lord does not call our attention so much to the outward conformity to any particular line of conduct, but rather
insists continually and emphatically upon the development of
the inward principle of *love* to God—a love that shall be *real*,
and that shall lead to a real surrender of our will *heartily* and
honestly to seek, and delight to please Him. *This* secured, the
conduct will follow, and the Lord be honored in all that we do.

There is many a man who is an ascetic in matters of eating,
and drinking, and dressing, but thoroughly selfish and unlovely
in the temper of his mind—un-Christlike in his home, and
uncharitable among his fellowmen. He is not at all separated
from the world, in the Christ-taught sense. There is many a
woman who would be shocked at the idea of going to a theatre,
or to a ball, or drinking wine, or playing cards, but who may
be thoroughly pharisaical in giving up these things, regarding
herself as better than others in doing it, and be in heart not at
all nearer to God by her thus abstaining from what indeed may
be properly considered as forms of worldliness and an injury to
spiritual life. But the *motive* in giving up these things may never
have been right. The heart may not be surrendered to God. The
will in *other things* may not be sanctified. An unhappy temper
is not curbed; a jealous disposition not resisted; selfishness in
little things not sought to be overcome; and the daily home-
life is made unhappy for herself and those around her. With all
that she thinks she has given up of the world, she is essentially
a worldly woman; for she cannot be said to be a Christ-like
woman. Our Lord might say of such: "These ought she to have
done, and not to leave the other undone."[1]

1 Matthew 23:23.

So let us be careful in laying down rules, and setting up *our conscience* as the standard of judgment for our fellow-believers, where the Word of God gives no *specific* directions, but leaves to the individual the application of *general principles*.

Where there is the true union based upon affection and confidence between husband and wife, a husband never would think of *writing out rules* as to how the wife was to act in her association with *one class* of people who were his avowed enemies, and who despised him and his ways; and towards *another class* who were his avowed friends, and loved him and his ways. The love in the heart of the wife would settle all that. The husband would simply have to say, "My dear, such a class are my enemies; and such a class are my friends. I leave it entirely to you what your attitude shall be towards them. My enemies may show you attentions, and invite you to their places of pleasure and enjoyment. They will never invite *me* with you. They do not wish my presence. They do not expect that you—if you associate with them—should speak of me, or regret my absence. I cannot lay down definite instructions for you, not to recognize them at all. There are times and places where you must needs meet them, and it is my desire that you should show them kindness in all ways consistent with honor to my name. I leave it to *your affection entirely*, as to the nature of your association with them."

So Christ has left His Church upon this earth with the message, "Ye know that the world hated Me;"[1] and "They hated Me without a cause."[2] "As the Father hath sent Me into the world, even so have I also sent you into the world."[3] Continue ministering to them in My name. Show them kindness and love. "Love your enemies; do good to them that hate you; and pray

---

1 See John 15:18.
2 John 15:25.
3 See John 20:21.

for them that despitefully use you and persecute you."[1] Try and win them to better thoughts of Me, your Lord and Master, and seek to bring them to accept My love for them. But, in all your relations to them, remember you are My Bride, My loved and chosen one. I leave to you the honor of My name. Let that name "be glorified in you,"[2] as "ye shine as lights in the world, holding forth the Word of life."[3] Shall not this confidence of Christ in the affection of His Bride *be honored*, so far as the reader is concerned?

May God give grace, and may the love of Christ be shed abroad in the heart by the Holy Ghost, that we may be of those who shall "count all things but loss for the excellency of the knowledge of Christ Jesus our Lord,"[4] and be found joyfully marching up *in line* in the ranks of the noble procession whose spiritual vision has pierced beyond the clouds of this world, and beheld "a city which hath foundations, whose maker and builder is God,"[5] and with their eyes upon that city have "confessed that they were strangers and pilgrims on the earth."[6]

Let us not expect or look for anything contrary to the Word of our Lord, "in the world ye shall have tribulation,"[7] or to be anything else on this earth but *strangers* and *pilgrims*, during this period of the rejection of Christ.

Let not the young disciple be deceived. The world *is still* the enemy of God, and of His Christ. There is not a nation on earth that would vote intelligently today for Christ to come and reign. The advance of *civilization* over the globe is *not Christianity*,

1 Matthew 5:44.
2 See 2 Thessalonians 1:12.
3 Philippians 2:15, 16.
4 Philippians 3:8.
5 Hebrews 11:10.
6 Hebrews 11:13.
7 John 16:33.

but, in many of its features is most decidedly antagonistic and opposed to Christianity, and is plainly spoken of in the Word of God as a preparation for the Anti-Christ, who will be permitted for a time to persecute God's people, and then "be consumed with the spirit of His mouth, and destroyed with the brightness of His coming" (2 Thessalonians 2:8).

Our Savior has plainly told us what the condition of the world shall be at His second coming. "As it was in the days of Noah, so shall it be also in the days of the Son of Man" (Luke 17:26). "And take heed to yourselves, lest at any time your hearts be overcharged with surfeiting, and drunkenness, and cares of this life, and so that day come upon you unawares. For as a snare shall it come on all them that dwell on the face of the whole earth. Watch ye therefore, and pray always, that ye may be accounted worthy to escape all these things that shall come to pass, and to stand before the Son of Man" (Luke 21:34–36).

And so the attitude of every child of God is to continue to be that of the saints in Thessalonica, towards "this present evil world;" for, although the end is near, the Lord is not yet come.

"Ye turned to God from idols, to serve the living and true God; and to wait for His Son from Heaven, whom He raised from the dead, even Jesus, which delivered us from the wrath which is coming" (1 Thessalonians 1:9, 10, lit.).

If we keep in this attitude, and where we can sincerely offer the Spirit-taught prayer of Revelation 22:20: "Amen: even so come, Lord Jesus," the last prayer in the Bible, we shall be kept separate from the world.

2 PETER 1:10, 11, 16—*Wherefore the rather, brethren, give diligence to make your calling and election sure: for if ye do these things, ye shall never fall. For so an entrance shall be ministered unto you abundantly into the everlasting kingdom*

of our Lord and Savior Jesus Christ . . . For we have not followed cunningly devised fables, when we made known unto you the power and coming of our Lord Jesus Christ, but were eyewitnesses of His majesty.

2 PETER 3:10–14—*But the day of the Lord will come as a thief in the night; in the which the heavens shall pass away with a great noise, and the elements shall melt with fervent heat, the earth also and the works that are therein shall be burned up. Seeing then that all these things shall be dissolved, what manner of persons ought ye to be in all holy conversation and godliness; looking for and hasting unto the coming of the day of God, wherein the heavens being on fire shall be dissolved, and the elements shall melt with fervent heat! Nevertheless we, according to His promise, look for new heavens and a new earth, wherein dwelleth righteousness. Wherefore, beloved, seeing that ye look for such things, be diligent that ye may be found of Him in peace, without spot, and blameless.*

FOR I AM NOW READY

(2 TIMOTHY 4:6, 7)

Attune your harps, ye heav'nly choir,
    On high the joy proclaim,
Of one for whom "to live" was "Christ,"
    For whom "to die" was "gain."

The "chief of sinners" Christ has sav'd,
    And as He homeward brings
This wondrous trophy of His love,
    The willing captive sings.

Ye saints on earth the words attend,

Oh, may they thrill each heart,
That we with zeal our race may run,
And sing when we depart.

May we, as dead to things below,
In Christ, our Saviour, live;
And when by Him we, too, are called,
May we this witness give.

Chapter 10

CONFORMITY TO THE WORLD

Be not conformed to this world; but be ye transformed by the renewing of your mind.—ROMANS 12:2.

t a weekly prayer meeting, where "Separation from the world, and consecration to God," had been presented as the topic for consideration, a gentleman related the following experience:

"I came to this city several years ago a professing Christian. I was a member of such a church, a regular attendant at the prayer meeting, a teacher in the Sunday school, and maintained daily worship in my family. But gradually I became engrossed in business; and the ambition to be rich took possession of me. I gave up my Sunday school class—too tired when Sunday came to attend to it; and the prayer meeting was neglected for the same reason. Soon family worship was also dropped, and I went on for some years a merely nominal Christian, attending church on Sunday, but without any real communion with God, and without any real happiness of soul. God often spoke to me, and I expected His chastening hand to come in some way. At last it came. I had but one child—a little daughter, the idol of my heart. One evening I was unexpectedly at home. My business usually occupied my evenings, and I was very little with my family; and they had not looked for my coming. My little daughter, much to my annoyance, was absent; and when her mother told me she had permitted her to go into a neighbor's for an hour, I was unreasonably angry, and sent for her, and declared that if she went there again I should punish her.

"Several weeks after this I was again unexpectedly at home; and again my little girl was away. My wife was much troubled in having to tell me that, being quite sure that I had no real objection to her going into our neighbor's, where she was under the very best influence—and not thinking I should be home—she had allowed her to go. I sent for the little girl, and chastised her. Just before going to her room she came, and between her sobs, said, 'Papa, I am sorry I disobeyed you. I thought perhaps you would be willing if mamma was. And Mr. Smith prays with his children every night; and I went in to pray for you, papa.' I choked, but could not say a word, as I kissed and sent her away. The next day my little girl was laid up with scarlet fever; and in three weeks I followed her little body to the grave. I came back to the house, I trust, a humbled, chastened man. My family altar was again erected, my place in the prayer meeting again filled; and, by God's help, I purpose henceforth to live for Him. But, my friends, my getting into the world, and what it has cost me, is a sad memory. May God lead you to accept His will without waiting for the discipline."

How many a child of God could give a similar experience, and tell of the bitterness of soul that has come from going down into the world! The Word of God must be our guide, and be *fully followed*, if we would be safe. Paul's position is the position for all who would have the victory over the world. "The world is crucified unto me, and I unto the world."[1] Made dead,

1 Galatians 6:14.

or set one side in the place of shame. The world cannot get to us without passing the Cross. This it will never do. And we are safe from the world if the Cross is kept between us and it. We, on the other hand, can only get to the world by passing the Cross; and this to our humbling, be it said, our carnal nature has often led us to do. We have given up the world; and yet we cling to it. We have known that we should avoid its temptations; and yet we have been inclined to get near enough to *peek* and see what they were: like a boy who could not go to the circus, but climbed a tree to see the procession.

Our rule should be, not to see how *near* we can live to the world and still keep the name of Christian, but, on the contrary, to keep *just as far away as possible*, "avoiding the appearance of evil." Not praying "lead us not into temptation,"[1] and then going right into temptation with our eyes open. The pilot of a United States revenue cutter was asked if he knew all the rocks along the coast where he sailed. He replied, "No; it is only necessary to know where there are no rocks." There could not be a more excellent answer to a soul troubled by trying to decide, from day to day, as to *what is*, and *what is not* conformity to the world. Wholehearted consecration to Christ, and the settled purpose to please Him in all things, will bring us into deep water where there are no rocks. *Half*-heartedness and *policy*, which Thomas Fuller says, "consists in serving God in such a manner as not to offend the devil," takes the soul into *very shallow* water indeed, with rocks on every hand.

O my brother, get out into the channel, and keep there. You will steer straight if you will keep "looking unto Jesus;" and the blood-red buoys anchored along the track will show you where there is deep water. Do not venture to leave the course that they mark, however tortuous the channel or winding your way: you

1 Matthew 6:13.

will surely run aground if you try to make short cuts. And do not think you gain by keeping near the *edge* of the channel. The *middle* is the safest, and where you will make the easiest progress. "How near could you drive my carriage to the edge of a precipice?" was the question asked by a gentleman to various applicants for the position of coachman. Different distances, all *perilously near*, were given. At last, a careful-looking man said, "Sir, I should keep just as far from it as the road would allow." "You are my man," was the reply; and the *adventurous* applicants were dismissed.

Surely, we can see the wisdom of this. Why cannot we see like wisdom in being *out and out Christians,* and keeping *as far from* the spirit of the world as possible as we pass on our way through it. There is really no consistency in drawing the line *at all* as Christians, only as we draw it, or rather recognize it as already drawn *for us*, according to God's Word. "Have *no fellowship* with the unfruitful works of darkness" (Ephesians 5:11). "The very God of peace sanctify you *wholly*" (1 Thessalonians 5:23). "Love not the world, neither *the things that are in the world. . . .* For *all* that is in the world, the lust of the flesh, and the lust of the eyes, and the pride of life, is not of the Father, but is of the world" (1 John 2:15, 16). "Wherefore come out from among them, *and be ye separate*, saith the Lord" (2 Corinthians 6:17).

The folly of trying to draw a line between things distinctively worldly and godless, *some* of which a Christian can consistently retain, and *others* which he ought to give up, is shown by the remark of a fashionable lady, who, as a professed Christian, had had her attention called to the fact that there was so little marked difference between Christians and the world. She admitted it, and upon reflection said, "Yes, certainly there should be *some* difference. We have been just like the world; and I am determined from this time to make a distinction. I shall give up *French opera.*" English and Italian, with theatres, balls, and other adjuncts of a fashionable life, she retained.

Any compromise must in the very nature of the case partake of something of the same absurdity. It is very doubtful whether this lady succeeded even in keeping away from French opera. The only way by which she could succeed would be to get out of its atmosphere by an *entire* consecration to God, and a coming *clean out* from all worldliness of spirit by a living fellowship with a living Savior. If asked upon what ground she gave up French opera, she would probably say to please God, who taught us in His Word to be *separate from the world.* What consistency could there then be with this premise established, and one's obligation to please God *recognized*, in retaining *anything* distinctively worldly? Like all attempts to compromise with evil in the individual heart and life, it was scripturally indefensible, and could lead to nothing permanently good in results.

The writer would most earnestly and affectionately urge upon young converts to treat this subject with careful and solemn reflection, and to be on their guard constantly against those influences around about them that would lead them into conformity to the world. The temptations will come from unexpected quarters, and with fearful power.

The ambition of parents and relatives will often lead them to urge a young woman to give herself in marriage to a godless man, whose only claim is his position and possessions in this world. A young man, from the same ambition, or foolishly allowing himself to be ensnared by outward attractions, will marry an unconverted woman, and be dragged along into the world—becoming a *worldling* with the worldling he has married or her unhappy attendant into the godless society she loves.

The evil of a Christian man or woman uniting themselves

in marriage to one who is not in sympathy with them in having Christ, and being willing to live for Christ, cannot be exaggerated. "How *can* two walk together unless they be agreed?" Dear young people do not treat this lightly. The *most solemn act of life* is the entering the marriage relation. Pray much over any decision you are called to make in reference to it. The large number of Christians who are led into the world, and lose their testimony for Christ in this way; the unhappy homes all around us; the unhappy wives and mothers we meet on every hand; the increasing prevalence of divorce and disgraceful separation— lead us to speak most earnestly upon this subject. You incur a fearful risk in letting inclination lead you into disobedience to God in this matter. Do not be deceived. If your influence over a person you love is not sufficient to lead them to Christ *before* marriage, you have no reason to expect that it will be *after* marriage.

A young Christian woman of B—— was sought in marriage by a thorough man of the world. She entertained his proposals, though warned by a faithful pastor of her danger. She was confident that after she was married she should succeed in turning him to God. He had promised her that he would try and be a Christian if she would marry him. The marriage took place; and the week after the young wife called to talk with her pastor about going to the theatre with her husband. He very much wished her to go, and promised, if she would go with him to *the theatre*, he would come with her to the *prayer-meeting*. Again she was faithfully told that her influence for good over her husband must come from constant *adherence* to her principles, and not in weakly yielding them. She, notwithstanding, *did* yield, and accompanied her husband. He *never* came with her to the prayer-meeting; and after a short time her own attendance ceased, and she soon gave up all hope that she was a Christian, and entered with her husband upon a life of worldly dissipation, which terminated, after a few years, in a most unhappy separation.

It is a great trial to young Christians to be looked upon as *"saints"* or *"peculiar* and *old-fashioned"* and to be *sneered at* or *laughed at* by those around them—the little circle that constitutes their world. But, this is just the cross-bearing that we of the *present* generation are called upon to suffer for Christ. In *other* generations it has been the faggot, the sword, and the rack. In ours, it is the resisting of one's flesh and blood, and the opposition from those who themselves profess the *name* of Christ, that constitutes the greatest trial of the thoroughly-in-earnest disciple.

A young lady in a fashionable home had been brought to Christ, and had been enabled for some years, amid much opposition, to faithfully witness for Him. The attention she attracted by refusing to do what she considered dishonoring to her Lord, and by her speaking of Christ to her unconverted friends, was often painful to her; and once, when repulsed and wounded in an effort of this kind, she for a time lost heart, and felt she should have to give up being a *consecrated* Christian. Just at this time she was invited to visit friends whom she had never seen, and who knew but little of her; and she resolved, that while there she would not openly speak of her Savior, or put herself in a position to be noticed as peculiarly religious. Her visit passed away; and, not happily to herself, she was enabled to keep her resolution. Upon the day of her leaving for home, a most attractive and accomplished lady, a fashionable woman of society, while walking alone with her, suddenly asked her, "Where is your sister, and why did she not come here? I mean your *religious* sister, the one who is known as the 'religious Miss J.' It was because I heard that she was to be here that I too accepted an invitation to come and spend the holiday. I am tired of the empty, unsatisfying, life I am leading, and have longed to talk with a real Christian."

With shame and confusion the faithless witness was obliged to confess that she had no sister; that she was the one who had been sometimes called the "religious Miss J.," and that *shame* of the badge, that should have been borne gladly for her Savior, had kept her silent. A precious opportunity to lead a weary soul to the Master had been lost. But let us trust the lesson was not in vain; and that a *fresh* consecration was witnessed, with an increased devotion manifested from the experience thus sadly gained. "It is a small matter with me to be judged of man's judgment,"[1] said the faithful Apostle. Would to God we could all as truthfully say the same! If we *saw Christ* as he did, we could. "To be approved of Christ" was his burning, consuming ambition. With this in view he did not care what the world thought of him. Why *should* he? And why should we? One is our Master, even Christ.

May grace be given to each of us to *know* Him, and to enter into the joyous devotion of the Apostle, who, knowing Christ, gladly surrendered all to Him, and gloried in saying, "Whose I am, and whom I serve."[2] "For *me* to *live* is Christ."[3] A dear companion of the writer, for three years a true yoke-fellow in Evangelistic work, one extremely cold winter evening, as he joined him in a railway train, to take his last journey on earth in the service of his Master, said pleasantly, "I got a good illustration from the man at the gate as I came on to the train. It is very cold, and every one was grumbling, and some abusing him, as he made them all get their tickets out and show them before

---

1 See 1 Corinthians 4:3.

2 Acts 27:23.

3 Philippians 1:21.

they could get past. I said to him, 'You don't seem to be very popular around here.' 'If I am popular with the man that put me here it is all that I want,' was his reply." "Ah," said this dear friend, "if we could go through this world, keeping the same thought towards Christ, what a straight path we should make!"

"Popular with one Man." May this be our ambition, the only ambition the Gospel enjoins. "Wherefore also we are *ambitious,* whether at home or absent, to be well-pleasing unto *Him*" (2 Corinthians 5:9. R. V. margin).

If we please Him we cannot please the world; and if we please the world we cannot please Him.

Dear child of God, which is your ambition?

I'VE NOW TO PLEASE BUT ONE

"From all its cares my heart retires,
    I've now to please but One;
Though deep and boundless my desires,
    I've now to please but One.
My will to Him I gladly bow,
With Him is all my business now,
Myself at His dear feet laid low:
    I've now to please but One.

"Christ is my way, my truth, my life,
    I've now to please but One;
The end of sorrow, doubt, and strife,
    I've now to please but One.
My Lord, in love I look to Thee,
Child-like attend what Thou wilt say,
Go forth and toil while yet 'tis day,
    I've now to please but One.

"Redeemed and saved by Christ the Lord,

I've now to please but One;
He bought me with His precious blood,
    I've now to please but One.
Out of this world by Jesus drawn,
My eye on Him, and Him alone,
In simple trust I follow on:
    I've now to please but One.

"In this my happy lot is cast,
    I've now to please but One;
In gardens fair, or deserts waste,
    I've now to please but One.
Though shame and poverty be mine,
Or prosperous suns upon me shine.
On Jesus I will still recline:
    I've now to please but One."

Chapter 11

THE FLESH

For I know that in me (that is, in my flesh) dwelleth no good thing.
—ROMANS 7:18.

Have no confidence in the flesh.—PHILIPPIANS 3:3.

hese passages are both applied to a believing, regenerated man. None but a regenerated man could know, or would admit the statement of the *first* passage; and none but a regenerated man could obey the exhortation of the *second*. The truth implied in the passages is very important, for it establishes the fact that there is *inside* the Christian man the existence of an enemy; and an enemy *inside* the citadel is far more dangerous than an enemy *outside*. And if that enemy can *disguise* himself, or hide his real character so as to be treated *as a friend*—like Hushai with Absalom—the more dangerous does he become. Happy is that man who has learned of the evil of his own heart enough to be afraid of and distrust himself. The wisest words Mr. Moody ever uttered were, "The worst man that ever crossed my path is D. L. Moody, the old man. I have had more trouble with him than with all the world beside." Every child of God knows what this means—or *will* know before his life is over—and can heartily say the same of himself or herself.

The *flesh* is the most dangerous enemy the new man has to contend with—always has been, and always will be. Bunyan's "Holy War" describes his insidious approaches and his entrance through "eye gate" and "ear gate" into the citadel of the Soul, and the havoc there wrought by his entrance. How important that the young Christian should be able to *recognise* and *identify* this enemy, and be warned from making *any truce* or coming to *any terms* with him. Like the warfare of the children of Israel with Amalek that was to never cease, but to continue unto the *latest* generation; so the Christian must war *continually* against *the flesh*. If he spare it, as Saul the king did Agag, permitting him to walk delicately, and say, "Surely the bitterness of death is past" (1 Samuel 15:32)—then he may be sure that *the flesh* will rob him of his crown, even as an Amalekite robbed Saul upon the field of Gilboa (2 Samuel 1:8–10).

That the believer may identify and know the nature of this enemy, and be on his guard against him, it is simply necessary to follow the teaching of the Word of God, and see him as there described from Genesis to Revelation, called in various places, "The first man," "The first Adam," "The old man," "The natural man," "Evil generation," "Corruption," "The flesh," "Me," "I." All meaning the corrupt human nature we all possess.

Let the reader carefully read the following passages and *see himself* in his corrupted humanity, inherited from a fallen progenitor (in whose fall the *fountain* of man's being was poisoned), through a long line of sinful ancestors, whose individual lives have swollen the stream of wickedness that now flows through his own veins. Genesis 5:1–3; 6:5 and 13; Psalm 53:1–3; Isaiah 1:4–6; 64:6; Jeremiah 17:9; Matthew 15:18, 19; 23:33; Romans 1:21–32; 3:9–18; 1 Corinthians 2:14; Galatians 5:19–21; Ephesians 2:1–3.

Let not the reader be deceived upon this subject. His own natural heart of conceit, and pride, and vanity, will be at enmity with this description. *The flesh does not like to be photographed by God's Word in its true characteristics.* Like the unknown murderer in Berlin, who at each effort of the officers to photograph him so worked and distorted his features that the resemblance was a very imperfect one; so the flesh tries to disguise its evil propensities and cover up its real properties by culture, or by forms of religion affecting simply the outward appearance, and not touching or changing the inward man, whose identity ever remains, for "that which is born of the flesh is flesh."

Nicodemus, to whom the words, "that which is born of the flesh is *flesh,*" were spoken, had to recognize his photograph there in the "Rogues' Gallery," with all the rest of us of the family of Adam. And it was only by admitting that it was he himself, that he could have part in the salvation sent by God for *sinners*—and for none else.

"I see the doctrine. It certainly *is* in the Bible," said D'Aubigne, when a student at Geneva, to Robert Haldane, as the latter opened up to him the subject of man's corruption by nature, from the epistle to the Romans.

"Yes," said the faithful man of God, "you see it *in God's Word;* but do you now see it in your *own heart?*"

The arrow of conviction went home with this question; and the young student was led to Christ.

In contrast with these passages, describing the family of the *first Adam,* of *which all* who are born into this world are members, we would place for future reference and careful study the following passages describing the family of the *second Adam,* of *which none* are members until Jesus Christ is received into the heart as Lord and Savior. "As we (Christians) have borne the image of the *earthy,* we shall also bear the image of the *heavenly.*

The *first man* is of the earth, earthy; the *second man* is the Lord from heaven." So 1 Corinthians 15:47–50; see also John 3:3, 5; John 1:12–14, 16; James 1:18; 1 Peter 1:3, 23–25; Galatians 4:4–7.

Now, from these passages, we believe that the Word of God teaches that the work of the Holy Spirit in regeneration is not to change the nature of the flesh at all; but to implant *a new nature*—Christ formed within by the Holy Spirit, in the power of which the believer does indeed *deny* the flesh, and is no longer living as *minding* the flesh. But the flesh is still there, *unchangeably* evil *in its nature*, with no improvement to be looked for in it, and the safety of the believer consisting in keeping it in the place of death. "Putting on the Lord Jesus Christ, and making no provision for the flesh, to fulfil the lusts thereof" (Romans 13:14).

The failure to see this, must, in the nature of the case, place the child of God in distress and spiritual difficulty. He will either be resting in the idea that at conversion his flesh was *instantaneously changed*, and all of its evil desires and bad propensities for ever eradicated; or, he will believe that a change was *commenced* in the nature of the flesh, which is to go on until all sin is eradicated, and the flesh is made perfectly holy by the gradual work of sanctification.

Under the first theory, that I am practically and for ever delivered from the flesh—by its *nature being changed* in my regeneration, and that no sin is left in me—I shall not expect any *warfare* with it, and shall not regard it longer as an enemy. The danger of the position is obvious. The enmity of *the flesh*, the natural heart, *will* manifest itself, as the new-born soul is led by the Spirit to "deny ungodliness, and worldly lusts; and to live soberly, righteously, and godly, in this present world" (Titus 2:12). And *when* it manifests itself, and lustings towards evil are discovered in the heart, darkness of soul follows: and the tempted, or overcome one, seeing sin is still within, will either give up his hope altogether and abandon himself to the rule of sin, or will seek a *second* regeneration, as if the first had not been real; and with solemn vows never to sin again, will make a new start.

Holding the *same theory*, in this second start, that a genuine conversion changes the nature of the flesh, he is very soon again made painfully aware that sin *is* still in his members, and evil lustings in his heart; and he is *again* in despair. So he will go on in this way, if a real child of God, holding on to Christ, falling, and getting (as *he* thinks), born again at regular intervals, but having much unhappy spiritual experience, and being made a stumbling block to others by his repeated backslidings and denials of Christ.

This is the experience of one who is disposed to be *real* and *honest* with his own soul, and who takes God's view of what sin is. Unhappily, with the *real love of sin* that clings to our deceitful hearts, we are all *always in danger* of lowering the standard as to sin, and condoning its evil. So the young convert, who has been led to believe that there is no longer any sin in him, in the sense that all *the thoughts of his mind*, and *the desires of his heart*, are *perfectly pleasing* to God, is in terrible danger—when lustings to evil *do* arise in his heart—of not regarding them as sinful. He judges them by his own consciousness and feeling, instead of God's Word. He argues "God has taken away all evil and wrong desires from me, and given me a perfectly clean heart; and I have no sin. So this, that I so strongly *want* to do, cannot be sin. I am *wholly* led by the Spirit; and the Spirit must be leading me to do this." And the temptation is yielded to, and a life of self-deception and hypocrisy is entered upon; sin allowed, and sin indulged; and yet the profession kept up of being without sin.

So Satan has led deluded souls on to the commission of the foulest and blackest sins, of uncleanness and adultery, dishonesty and deceit, while still maintaining the Christian name. Most of those who have thus fallen, and who live in sin, are undoubtedly children of the devil, and were never anything else—"sows who quickly returned to their wallowing in the mire," for they were never anything *but sows*. "Dogs turned again to their own vomit,"[1] for they were never anything *but dogs*. Like Simon Magus, who *professed* belief and was baptized, they have "neither part nor lot with Christ—their heart is not right in the sight of God."[2]

But, mixed up with them, drawn away among them, are undoubtedly those who have been *truly* brought to Christ, and have been left to be overcome by sin, as was David, that, like him, they may correct their views as to the flesh; and, with him, agree fully with God's estimate of it, and learn, with Paul, to *have no confidence* in it.

Oh, dear young convert, how important it is that you should know the *evil of your own heart*, and be kept from false views as to perfection in the flesh or a profession of being without sin! Surely those who make such profession must have some other standard before them than the infinite requirements of God's holy law, both in what they should *do* and what they should *not* do, as illustrated in the life on earth of the only perfectly sinless One. *He* could *truly* say, with each day's setting sun, "I have lived a *perfect* life today. It could not under any circumstances have been *better*. I have left nothing undone. I have done perfectly what I have done."

But for erring, fallible man to say this! how *great* the blindness! how *awful* the sin! how dreadful the pride of heart it must

1 See 2 Peter 2:22.

2 Acts 8:21.

culminate in! The humble and the lowly draw near to God: and, "Thus saith the high and lofty One that inhabiteth eternity, whose name is Holy; I dwell in the high and holy place: with him also that is of a *contrite* and *humble* spirit, to revive the spirit of the humble, and to revive the heart of the contrite ones" (Isaiah 57:15).

The *best* day that the *best man or woman on earth* ever lived, would be closed—if the soul was in communion with God—with such a consciousness of much that *might* have been done to *make it better*, and much in motive or in manner of doing what *was* done that was *imperfect*, that there would be far more occasion for humbling confession and for seeking forgiveness through the great High Priest, than for boastful elation. And, how plain it is that, if the latter spirit be yielded to, the service of the day is marred, and there is no glory of the setting sun reflected along its horizon; for the flesh, exalted, has hidden Christ from view.

God has forgiveness and healing for those who confess their sins. But it is very difficult for the ordinary reader of the Word of God to find any place this side of Heaven for those, who have *no sins to confess*. And when one sees the delusions and darkness that come from their unscriptural teaching, the wish must often arise that they were speedily taken there; even as Paul, in his love for his dear converts who were being led away from the ground of acceptance as being wholly and only in Christ, and not in works of the flesh, was led to say, "I would they were even cut off which trouble you" (Galatians 5:12).

There is the second view of the *gradual* change of the flesh that we would briefly consider. It is not denied but that there may be, and is, the work of progressive sanctification in the experience of the believer, consisting, as we believe the Scriptures teach, in the increasing knowledge of the Lord Jesus as a personal living

Savior, and an increasing faith in Him to keep us *from* the evil of the flesh. But the important discrimination should be made, that this is not the *changing* of the evil nature of the flesh. The man in India with a pet tiger, seemingly very tame, and much of its native wildness subdued by discouraging influences, found, to his sorrow, that its *nature* was still unchanged, as, with a taste of human blood, it again sought human life.

A venerable Christian man, for years an honored teacher of theology in a leading college, where he had defended the view that progressive sanctification was the gradual taking out of the nature of the flesh, its evil attributes and characteristics, until it, the flesh, was holy and without sin, was in much spiritual dark ness before his death, and said, "Either one of two things is true. First, the view that I have always held that, at regeneration, a progressive work of sanctification is commenced, which is to go on by the power of the Holy Spirit until all the evil in the nature of the flesh is taken away in this life is *wrong.* Or, second, I have never been regenerated. The evil characteristics of the flesh are still with me, still burdening me, still humbling me." Ultimately he believed he had been wrong in his view; and that the work of the Holy Spirit in sanctification did not change the *nature* of the flesh, any more than it did in *regeneration.*

Now it is of the utmost importance to a believing man to see this. If the Word of God teaches that "in *me*, in *my flesh*, dwelleth no good thing," and teaches it in connection with other passages, that makes it clear that no good thing ever will dwell in it, or come from it; but that, when allowed to act, it will act out its nature, which is unchangeably evil—then it must be that those who for years have prayed, and toiled, and fasted, and denied the flesh, with the expectation of changing its nature, must of necessity be thrown into darkness of soul, as they sadly find that the result they *expected* to attain—namely, *annihilation of all evil* in the flesh, and a consciousness of *perfect* sinlessness and *perfect* purity—has not been reached.

In view of these, and other difficulties that might be presented, it will be seen that a Christian should have right and clear views of his relations, as a believer, to the flesh. Indeed, it would seem impossible for him to be kept in peace and to grow in faith unless he is on right and Scriptural lines in this matter. It is vain to tell a convert as a poorly-taught Christian once did, "Oh, you just let the old man alone; do not bother yourself about him." He received the apt reply: "Ah, but there is just the trouble; he won't let me alone." The clamoring of the flesh, its selfishness, vanity, pride, jealousy, love of ease, cowardice, and conceit, come into painful prominence in his consciousness as the Spirit of God shows him what he is; and the harder he struggles, the more prominent they seem. He is in despair unless he finds an explanation of this conflict that will not destroy his hope, and a deliverance that is based upon *truthfulness*. Such an explanation the Word of God gives, and such a deliverance it presents.

Jesus Christ is the Savior of His people, and does save them *from* their sins—*real sins*, not make-believe ones; *vile* sins (for *all* sin is vile—it is vile to sin in any way against a holy God); hell-deserving, soul-defiling sins. Blessed be His name! He *is* the Savior from them all. The remedy in all things for a believer, is to know Christ.

CHILD OF JESUS, OFT DEPRESSED

Child of Jesus, oft depressed,
    Yielding to thy doubts and fear,
In thy trials sore distressed,
    Fainting for some word of cheer;

Come, thy need is all supplied,
    Take by faith what God doth give:
Believe that you in Christ have died,
    Believe that you in Him now live.

Often weary, often weak,
    Foes without and fears within;
Knowing not what path to take,
    To escape from *self* and sin:
In thy *risen Saviour* hide,
    From Him *risen life* receive;
Believe that you in Christ have died,
    Believe that you in Him now live.

Sorrowing oft, and often sad,
    As thy failures thou dost scan;
Selfish aims those failures made,
    Now let Jesus lead and plan.
Let the Spirit ever guide,
    Let the flesh no more deceive;
Believe that you in Christ have died
    Believe that you in Him now live.

Chapter 12

FLESH AND SPIRIT

The flesh lusteth against the spirit, and the spirit against the flesh.
—GALATIANS 5:17.

In the same man, in the believing man, joined by one in generation to the first Adam joined by the other in regeneration to the second Adam. The one, corruptible in nature, poisoned by sin, and at enmity with God. The other, incorruptible in nature, untainted by sin, and loving God. And there the two natures abide. The Spirit does not, in *this life*, change flesh into spirit; and the flesh *cannot*, thank God, change the *spirit into flesh*. Nature never changes. It can be subdued, kept under, put in the place of death, denied, bruised, disciplined, chastened; but as long as a thing *lives*, its nature cannot be changed.

So, while man's life continues in the flesh, he will have the nature of the flesh; and, when regenerated, warfare with the flesh is inevitable, and must continue through life. If a man thinks he has got to a point in his experience, where the flesh has become changed in nature, and he *has* "confidence" in it, in the face of God's Word, which tells him to have *"no confidence"* in it, and ceases his watchfulness and warfare, he is certainly wrong, and will be rudely awakened from his delusion by some action of the flesh that will be terribly humbling, and lead him back to heartily take sides with God's estimate of it. So David was forced to say when he was suffered to fall, "Against Thee, Thee only, have I sinned, and done this evil in Thy sight; that Thou mightest be justified when Thou speakest, and be clear when Thou judgest. Behold, I was shapen in iniquity, and in sin did my mother conceive me" (Psalm 51:4, 5).

For proof texts, that the flesh and spirit are in the same man, and abide in him, unchanged in nature, while he lives on earth, see Romans 7:20 to 23: "Now if I do that I would not, it is no more I that do it, but sin that dwelleth in Me. I find then a law, that, when I would do good, evil is present with me. For I delight in the law of God after the inward man: but I see another law in my members, warring against the law of my mind, and bringing me into captivity to the law of sin which is in my members." Two opposing principles in the same man, and the *law* of their acting, laid down. That is, "the flesh" is in the regenerate man, and if he allows it to act, its action will be in accordance with its nature, in opposition to and in war with the Spirit of God. The remedy, as Paul gloriously brings out in the eighth chapter, is to so come into fellowship with Christ in His risen life, that we shall live in the Spirit, and not be brought under the power of the flesh. But the recognition of the presence of the flesh is clearly insisted upon, in the possibility of living after it, as presented in the 13ᵀᴴ verse, and in the exhortation in the same verse to "mortify the deeds of the body," which is addressed to believers.

In Galatians 5:16, 17, we have these words—"This I say then, Walk in the Spirit, and ye shall not fulfil the lust of the flesh. For the flesh lusteth against the Spirit, and the Spirit against the flesh; and these are contrary the one to the other: so that ye cannot do the things that ye would."

The presence of the flesh, and of its lusting in the believing man, is here recognized. The remedy is, not its annihilation, not its change of nature; but the same as in Romans 8—the practical fellowship of the soul with a personal Christ, by walking in the Spirit. And the promise is, that if I walk in the Spirit (*i.e.*, let the Holy Spirit have His way with me, in revealing Christ to my soul through the Scriptures, and yielding myself to God in obedience to the Word, as the Word reveals His will), "I shall not fulfil the lusts of the flesh," for "I cannot do the things that I would." The things that I would do are the things that would gratify the flesh. But if I am in real communion with God, I cannot do these things. The consciousness of His displeasure, to which a soul walking in the Spirit becomes more and more sensitive, is a cause of such grief and unhappiness that, above all things, we shall dread the being overcome by sin; and in this communion with God we shall be kept by Him from the power of sin. Sin will be in us, but "shall not have dominion over us,"[1] for we are not under law, but under grace. But this practical victory will only be realized just in proportion as we take the place given us in Galatians 3:13: "redeemed from the curse of the law"; and in Galatians 3:26: "children of God by faith in Christ Jesus"; in the place of sons, as Galatians 4:5 to 7: "standing fast in our liberty in Christ," no matter what the world, or the devil, or the flesh, may say, as in Galatians 5:1. So again, and continually, we would emphasize, Christ must first be seen, and accepted as our Redeemer, before we can know the work of the Spirit as our sanctifier.

It must also be kept clear in mind that the ground of our acceptance with God never changes. We stand *in Christ* all the way. Never in self, and never on the ground of my being perfect

1 See Romans 6:14.

in self, do I have access to God, or receive any blessing from God; but, always on the ground of having a perfect Savior. And just in proportion as I discover and confess my own imperfections, and appropriate Him as my sufficiency, do I have victory over the flesh.

So 1 John 1:8 to 10; 2:1 and 2—"If we say that *we have no sin*, we deceive ourselves, and the truth is not in us. If we confess our sins, He is faithful and just to forgive us our sins, and to cleanse us from all unrighteousness. If we say that *we have not sinned*, we make Him a liar, and His Word is not in us. My little children, these things write I unto you, that ye sin not. And *if any man sin*, we have an advocate with the Father, Jesus Christ the righteous: and He is the propitiation for our sins: and not for ours only, but also for the sins of the whole world."

He writes unto them of the fellowship that they are called to enjoy with the Father and with the Son, that in the faith of the fellowship they may be kept from sinning. But recognizing the possibility—through failure to walk in this fellowship, and by the flesh acting—of the child of God falling into sin, the advocacy of Christ as our High Priest in heaven before God is introduced, that the Christian with a condemning conscience may come to Him and receive cleansing and restoration, as typified by what the Jewish High Priest did for Israel when they were defiled.

Sin—past, present, and future—is recognized and provided for.

"If we say we have not sinned, we make Him a liar."

"If we say we have no sin, we deceive ourselves."

"If any man sin, we have an Advocate."

So not by a profession of perfection, and of being without sin, do I find peace and access to God: but by continued confession of imperfection, and seeing sin in all of its aspects—past, present, and future—fully provided for in the Blood.

The presence of the flesh—*i.e.*, the corrupt human nature in believers—John himself being included—is insisted upon in the 8ᵀᴴ verse: sin there meaning the nature or principle of sin; rather than the outward act, as in 9ᵀᴴ and 10ᵀᴴ verses, and also in 1ˢᵀ and 2ᴺᴰ verses of the second chapter.

The reader will also see that the fact that Jesus now bears the relation of High Priest to His Church on the earth, and, of course, to each and every member of it, involves that they of themselves must be imperfect and sinful as in the sight of God, and cannot possibly have access to God except through their High Priest. So Hebrews 5:1 and 2—"For every high priest taken from among men is ordained for men in things pertaining to God, that he may offer both gifts and sacrifices for sins: who can have compassion on the ignorant, and on them that are out of the way; for that he himself also is compassed with infirmity."

This office of High Priest the Scriptures clearly teach us Christ will continue to hold until His second coming, when His Church will be caught up from earth, and be glorified and presented in resurrection bodies, "without spot, or wrinkle, or any such thing." His High-priestly office is then laid aside, for it is no longer needed.

How great the error then, until that time, to profess an attainment in perfection, where I no longer need Christ in His priestly office.

It must be insisted upon that any interpretation of texts of Scripture that would put a child of God in a position out of harmony with this truth must be unsound.

1 John 3:9—"Whosoever is born of God doth not commit sin; for his seed remaineth in him: and he cannot sin, because he is born of God," is often thus used. What does it mean? That it cannot mean that everyone that is born of God is *sinless* is

obvious; for that would contradict 1 John 1:8 and 10. Is not the explanation found in considering *what it is* in a man that is born of God? It cannot be *the flesh* that is born of God, for our Lord says, "That which is born of the flesh *is flesh*, and that which is born of the Spirit *is spirit*"; and Ephesians 4:23 states the Holy Ghost in regeneration "renews us in the spirit of our minds." Therefore, the mind is the subject of it.

"The new birth," says an old writer, "is a new nature, created in the mind, which never existed in it before." It is conveyed by the Spirit of God. He is the Author of it. Hence, it is called after His name, spirit. It is contrary to every desire and propensity of the old man. There is no sin in *it*. Hence, the apostle says, "Whosoever is born of God doth not commit sin; for his seed remaineth in him: and he cannot sin because he is born of God" (1 John 3:9).

So the new birth does not change or alter the sinful nature and disposition which were inherent in the sinner when this new birth took place. That remains unchangeably evil to the last. So 1 John 1:8 and 10 are true of believers as to the existence of sin, and the fact of sinning, for *the flesh* is there; and 1 John 3:9 is also true, for the spirit is there. They have been made "partakers of the divine nature" (see 2 Peter 1:4); and the *divine nature* in the soul can no more sin in the believer than the divine nature in Heaven. It is plainly put before us in the Scripture that it is by virtue of the union of our spirit with the sinless, glorified, Son of God, "the first-born from the dead," that we have our acceptance as sinless ones before God; and never by virtue of our being sinless in ourselves. So, in Colossians 1:22, the believers to whom the apostle writes are said to be "presented holy, and unblameable, and unreproveable in His sight;" and in the second chapter, tenth verse, are declared "complete" in Christ. Yet these same believers, perfect in Christ, are also recognized as being on the earth in a fleshly nature, and are told in Colossians 3:5, to "mortify their members which are upon the earth," and are instructed specifically as to the denying of fleshly lusts in the third and fourth chapters.

Now, if Colossians 1:22 were to be taken as describing an actual state of perfection in the flesh attained by believers, what sense could there be in Colossians 3:5, and the succeeding verses of the epistle, clearly recognizing a state of things far from perfection?

And if there is a necessity here, in order to understand seeming contradictions of the Word, to admit that there is upon one side presented the perfect standing that a believer has, by virtue of his spiritual union with Christ, "translated into the Kingdom of the Son of His love" (13TH verse); "Christ formed within him, the hope of glory" (27TH verse); already, as in God's sight "risen with Christ" (3:1): and, on the other side, that the same believer has "members still upon the earth," united to a fleshly nature by being born of the flesh, as he is united to a spiritual nature by being born of the Spirit; and is warned against this fleshly nature, and told to mortify it and deny it: surely this is the key to an understanding of all similar presentations of kindred truth.

The Scriptures are in perfect harmony; and it is contrary to the mind of the Scripture, as well as opposed to sound sense, to make a theory upon isolated texts that contradict the general tenor of the Word as a whole.

If 1 John 3:9, and 1 John 3:6 its parallel passage, are taken as meaning a literal and absolute state of perfection and sinlessness, then they must be accepted as meaning this, that in every person truly born of God, every thought of the mind, every desire of the heart, every action of the body, is absolutely holy and perfect, and pleasing in the sight of a holy God; and if a regenerated person once fails in thus living in thought, desire, and act, "he

has not seen God, neither known Him." This is the statement of
the sixth verse. This is so utterly contrary to the teaching of our
Lord, and the recorded experience of Peter, and others whom the
Word tells us *were* born of God, that it cannot be accepted as the
true meaning of the passage: it proves too much.

Let not the young convert be led into such a position.
His own conscious experience will contradict his professions.
Victory over the power and dominion of sin, God indeed promises as we abide in Christ. But sin still wars within the soul, even
of a believer, and carries on a strife which justification does not
save him from, nor sanctification hinder; but rather the contrary: for, as believers, it is written of us: "Think it not strange
concerning the fiery trial which is to try you, as though some
strange thing happened unto you" (1 Peter 4:12).

"What shall we say then? shall we deny the existence of the
conflict, and argue for a perfection in the flesh, which every
confession of sin and prayer for forgiveness practically contradicts? Shall we talk wildly and unscripturally of sin being dead
within us, as well as crucified for us? Shall we, to suit the occasion, lower the standard of God's holy law, and alter the character of the believer's sin, as if, in his case, it was not *tenfold*
more sinful, if possible? Shall we extenuate trespass, because
found in a saint; and sympathize with the self-righteous com-
miseration not unfrequently expressed for those 'undeveloped
brethren' those 'half-instructed' Christians described as being
'still in the seventh, and not yet in the eighth of Romans'? Shall
we continue, from prejudice, to close our eyes to the patent
fact, that the conflicts and complaints of the seventh chapter are
acknowledged and repeated in the eighth chapter: 'Ourselves
also which have the first fruits of the Spirit, even we ourselves,
groan within ourselves, waiting for the adoption, to wit, the
redemption of our body.'"

"Not so; God forbid. But we will, with the Apostle, 'thank God through Jesus Christ our Lord,' for promised deliverance; and rest in the assurance that sin shall not have dominion over us, for we are not under the law, but under grace."[1]

My brother in Christ, be not cast down or discouraged at the existence of this warfare. Its very existence is an evidence of the presence of God's Spirit in your soul. "There hath no temptation taken you but such as is common to man" (1 Corinthians 10:13). Your safety lies in a humbling recognition and hearty belief in the truth of the statement of God's Word, that "in you, in your flesh, dwelleth no good thing," and a ceasing to expect that any good thing ever will dwell in it (that is, in its nature); and your danger lies in being led into a false profession of perfection and sinlessness in the flesh, and an application to yourself of words which only Jesus, as the only Sinless One that has ever walked this earth, could truthfully utter: "The prince of this world cometh, and hath nothing in Me."[2] Most earnestly and affectionately are you warned against this.

The Apostle Paul could say, "I exercise myself to have always a conscience void of offence" (Acts 24:16), and "I know nothing against (lit.) myself" (1 Corinthians 4:4, R.V.). Yet he expressly adds: "Yet am I not hereby justified; but He that judgeth me is the Lord." So, the believer is not to allow sin to rule him, but ever aim to have a good conscience in that which he allows. But he should always remember that the Lord's standard is infinitely higher than his; and that he cannot say he is without sin before God, even though conscience may not condemn. The same Apostle, whose attainments in holiness and sincere consecration to Christ were far beyond anything the world has ever

---

1 See LECTURES ON ROMANS VII. By Rev. M. Rainsford, Hamilton, Adams & Co., London.
2 John 14:30.

seen since, also clearly recognized the existence of the flesh, its evil characteristics, and his danger from it: "And lest I should be exalted above measure through the abundance of the revelations, there was given to me a thorn in the flesh, the messenger of Satan to buffet me, lest I should be exalted above measure" (2 Corinthians 12:7).

Now, without reference to what the "thorn" was, the point in this testimony is, that Paul had that in his flesh that was in danger of being exalted or puffed up by reason of the distinguished honor conferred upon him as an apostle; and the thorn was made necessary to keep him from being puffed up. The thorn is called "a messenger of Satan to buffet him." So Satan did come, and found something in Paul. In modern times, Paul, after such a testimony, would have been told that he had not trusted the Lord fully; or all that he felt in his flesh in danger of being proud, conceited, or vain, would have been taken out of him, and Satan would have found nothing in him. It was not taken out; but he was kept humble by his "thorn," and God's grace given him to live nearer to Christ than ever, as he felt his weakness and knew his danger.

"The creature is dead; but he don't know it," said an Irishman, as he looked at the moving legs of a turtle whose head he had cut off a few hours before. "The flesh is dead in me," says the modern opponent of Paul; but the lively motions of the flesh that are often seen by the onlooker make him doubt if the flesh knows it.

The remedy in all things for a believer is—to *know Christ*.

KEEP YOURSELVES IN THE LOVE OF GOD

The love of God outflowing
To lost and ruined men,

From God to man, through Jesus;
   Through Jesus, back again.
O Spirit, sent as teacher,
   Teach us this love to know,
That in God's love believing,
   Our love to Him may grow.

As sons, *in Christ*, God seats us
   At His right hand in heaven;
And there the Father's blessing
   Through Christ to us is given:
On Christ in glory gazing,
   As there He sits in grace,
In Him—oh, joy amazing!—
   We see the Father's face.

The Father seen in Jesus,
   Our life for evermore;
And God in Christ accepted,
   God truly we adore.
Thus, in the Spirit walking,
   All grace we find supplied
Our bodies to be yielding,
   With Jesus crucified.

The victory that o'ercometh
   We thus, by faith, do gain;
The faith that works by loving,
   That we from Christ obtain.
To *please* is love's ambition;
   To give up self, its joy;
Saved ones to serve their Saviour,
   Find nought but glad employ.

Chapter 13

IS THE FLESH DEAD?

He that is dead is freed from sin.—Romans 6:7.

"I have the Word of God for saying that it *is*," says the reader.

Galatians 5:24 says—*They that are Christ's have crucified the flesh with the affections and lusts.*

Romans 8:10—*If Christ be in you, the body is dead because of sin.*

Colossians 2:20—*Wherefore, if ye be dead with Christ.*

Colossians 3:3—*For ye are dead.*

Romans 6:2—*How shall we, that are dead to sin, live any longer therein?*

Romans 6:3, 4—*Know ye not that so many of us as were baptized into Jesus Christ were baptized into His death? Therefore we are buried with Him by baptism into death.*

So 5ᵀᴴ to 11ᵀᴴ verses. Every one of them has the word *dead* or *death* in them, as applied to the believer in Christ; and upon these verses I rest my doctrine, and obey the command of the eleventh verse: "Likewise reckon ye also yourselves *to be dead* indeed unto sin; but alive unto God, through Jesus Christ our Lord."

Well, this is a strong presentation, most certainly, of Scriptural authority for the doctrine that the flesh *is* dead; and the verses quoted must be prayerfully considered as to their meaning and intent. If they mean literally that when a man is born of God by the acceptance of Jesus Christ as his Lord and Savior, and trusts in the blood of Christ as shed for his sins, that that moment the flesh, with all of its evil desires, lustings, conceits, vanities, and hypocrisies, is *dead*, absolutely *dead*, and is never going to trouble the converted man any more—no more than the man in the grave troubles the man living in the house he once occupied—then certainly we are wrong in the expositions already given; and those who are conscious that the flesh is troubling them need to be converted: for, with this accepted as the teaching of the Word of God, it is obvious that if the flesh is not *actually dead* as to any motion of sin in the members or evil in the heart, they have not been really brought to the Lord. For, be it noted that these words are not spoken of a privileged class of believers, but of all believers. Now, the statement itself of all that this interpretation must claim, introduces a grave suspicion that this cannot be the meaning of these texts.

It will be noticed that all of them are taken from the writings of Paul. Therefore the experience of Paul should be duly weighed in determining his meaning, and his statements studied in connection with the argument he is presenting in the epistles where they occur. It will be noticed that he includes himself in the verses quoted in the sixth of Romans, in the pronouns "us" and "we," all the way through; as is his custom when speaking of the relation of believers to Christ. So, speaking of himself, he says he is dead with Christ, and that he is dead to sin.

Now, if he meant by this that sin had ceased to exist in him, and that the flesh was absolutely and practically dead, how can we understand the statement made in Romans 7:21 to 23?—"I find then a law that, when I would do good, evil is present with me. For I delight in the law of God after the inward man: but I see another law in my members, warring against the law of my mind, and bringing me into captivity to the law of sin which is in my members." That is, in the members of a *regenerated* man: for he is speaking of his own experience in his conflict with sin after his baptism into the death of Christ; and none but a regenerated man could be described as "delighting in the law of God." That point is settled by Romans 8:7, which plainly states that the unregenerate man is at enmity with the law of God. And how can we explain 2 Corinthians 12:7, where the life of the flesh is recognized as being that in Paul which might be puffed up in a God-dishonoring way?

Certainly we cannot accept an interpretation of the Apostle's words that places him in a position not only contradictory to his own teaching, but which his own recorded experience contradicts. He could not have meant to teach us—in the sense of which we are speaking—that the flesh is dead; and then have said of his experience as a believer, "So fight I, not as one that beateth the air; but I keep under my body, and bring it into subjection" (1 Corinthians 9:26, 27). Surely Paul was too matter-of-fact a man, and too sensible, to spend the time and energy described in these words upon that which was actually dead.

There must have been a line of truth in the mind of the Apostle, an understanding of which will explain his words without these contradictions.

That truth it is not difficult to find. It is the central truth of the Gospel. Paul was pervaded with it, saturated with it; and is continually reiterating it in one way or another. Christ's death, in the place of and for the sinner, accepted as the sinner's death judicially by God. It is this that sets the sinner free.

It is on the ground that death is past and judgment met, that he is made a child of God. How could Paul, and how can any intelligent believer ever cease presenting it? Each passage that has been quoted as to the flesh being dead, has its explanation right here. As in God's sight, in my judicial relation to His law, *I am dead:* "Christ is the end of the law for righteousness to *every one* that believeth" (Romans 10:4).

"I am (have been, Gr.) crucified with Christ; nevertheless I live: yet not I, but Christ liveth in me; and the life which I now live in the flesh I live by the faith of the Son of God, who loved me, and gave Himself for me" (Galatians 2:20). "I, through the law, am *dead to the law*, that I might live unto God" (Galatians 2:19). It is indeed the blessed privilege of every believer to know that, in the death of Christ on Calvary's Cross as his Substitute he died; and that he now is dead, and judgment past. But that, as a fact to be believed, and rested in upon the authority of God's Word, is one thing; and the taking of the passages of the Word that state this fact, and endeavor to show from them that the flesh is practically dead, and the believer actually sinless while living in the flesh, is quite another thing.

With Galatians 2:19—"I am dead to the law," look at Galatians 5:24—"They that are Christ's have crucified the flesh;" and one statement explains the other. Having accepted Christ, and seen myself nailed to the Cross in His person, I should now live as one who, by the Cross, is set free from the law as to penalty, and from the law of sin in my members. As a man set free, I can claim that sin shall not have dominion over me, and, walking as a free man, "standing fast in the liberty

wherewith Christ hath made me free," I shall not fulfil the lusts
of the flesh (Galatians 5:1, 16; Romans 13:14).

But that Galatians 5:24 does not mean that the flesh is actually dead; and, as dead, to give no more trouble—which, we
must insist, a thing dead cannot do—this verse, following after
it, is conclusive. "Brethren, if a man be overtaken in a fault, ye
which are spiritual restore such an one in the spirit of meekness;
considering thyself, lest thou also be tempted." Paul certainly
did not seem to consider it as calculated to cultivate the spirit
of meekness—to instruct converts to profess that the flesh was
dead; in the sense that Satan might come, and he would find
nothing in them.

Romans 8:10 is connected with the argument that turns
upon the first verse of the chapter, and runs back to the fourth
verse of the seventh chapter, where we are clearly told how the
body is dead. "Ye also are become dead to the law by the body of
Christ; that ye should be married to another, even to Him that
is raised from the dead—that ye should bring forth fruit unto
God." So in union with Christ I died as under law; and by that
death I am free from law, that by spiritual union with Jesus as a
risen Savior I may live a spiritual life, governed by the law of the
spirit, and not by the law of the flesh.

The exhortation of the 13ᵀᴴ verse—"For if ye live after the
flesh (i.e., ruled by it) ye shall die; but, if ye through the Spirit
do mortify the deeds of the body, ye shall live"—is conclusive
that the words of the 10ᵀᴴ verse, "the body is dead," cannot be
taken as meaning that the nature of the flesh is changed, or that
the flesh is practically dead; for how can a body that is dead be
mortified?

Colossians 2:20 and 3:3 we have already used in connection with Colossians 3:5—"Mortify therefore your members
which are upon the earth"—as showing that the epistle cannot

be harmonized in its statements, without the same exposition that the death refers to the believer's judicial relations to the law in Christ's death, as his substitute; in the faith of which he is united to a living Christ, and therefore is called upon to "mortify the flesh" in which he still lives, and to "put off the old man, with his deeds," in the sense of not one putting off once for all, but a daily denying of the flesh in the minding of the Spirit: "Always bearing about in the body the dying of the Lord Jesus, that the life also of Jesus might be made manifest in our body. For we which live are alway delivered unto death for Jesus' sake, that the life also of Jesus might be made manifest in our mortal flesh" (2 Corinthians 4:10, 11).

There certainly could not be a daily denying of the flesh if the flesh were once for all dead. We do not need to guard against a dead enemy. And if the flesh has to be denied by the believer, it must live; and if it lives, its nature lives, unchangeably evil and opposed to the Spirit of God.

Romans 6:2 is connected in the Apostle's argument with Romans 3:24, 25, where the sole ground of a sinner's justification before the law is declared to be "redemption in Christ Jesus," received "through faith in His blood," a truth further developed in Romans 4:25—"Who was delivered for our offences, and was raised again for our justification." "Christ died for the ungodly" (verse 6). "Christ died for us" (verse 8). "When we were enemies, we were reconciled to God by the death of His Son, much more, being reconciled, we shall be saved by His life." Then, in its connection, comes the practical question of Romans 6:1—"Shall we continue in sin, that grace may abound?" answered, as every man who knows the fullness and freeness of God's redeeming love in Christ would be constrained to answer: "God forbid. How shall we, that are dead to sin, live any longer therein? Know ye not that as many of us as were baptized into Jesus Christ were baptized into His death?"

The "dead to sin" is explained by its connection with baptism "into *His death.*" It is not "dead to sin" in the sense of being dead to the sense of its presence, but dead to its condemnation and penalty. "Knowing this, that our old man is (*lit.* was) crucified with Him," and "He that is dead is justified (margin) from sin" (verses 6 and 7). The effect of my seeing myself thus delivered in the death of my Savior will certainly be to lead me to walk in newness of life, and to cease from living in sin; and I am, indeed, called upon in the 11ᵀᴴ verse, in view of this deliverance, to "likewise reckon myself also to be dead indeed unto sin, but alive unto God, through Jesus Christ our Lord."

Two words are noteworthy. First, *"likewise"* connecting *how* I am to consider myself dead unto sin, with the statement in the 10ᵀᴴ verse that Christ "died unto sin once." Now His death unto sin was not the ceasing from sin in the flesh, for He had no sin in the flesh, but refers to His actual death as an atonement for sin on the Cross; and the exhortation is, *"likewise* reckon ye yourselves dead." Surely it is here, as ever where similar words are used, that we should see ourselves dead in a crucified Savior, who died in our stead, and on our behalf. "Reckon" yourselves dead, and "reckon" yourselves alive unto God in (Gr.) Jesus Christ our Lord; *i.e.,* live in the faith of it; and "Let not sin therefore reign in your mortal bodies, that ye should obey it in the lusts thereof." So, is the flesh dead? *Yes,* and *No.*

YES, praise God, judicially, as under penalty of God's law, it *is* dead. "The wages of sin is death:" and Christ has taken the wages for all His believing people. "I am crucified with Christ;" and "He that believeth is passed from death unto life." Faith is to reckon this as so, on the authority of God's own Word.

NO, as to the existence of the nature of the flesh in the believer. The flesh is *not* dead, and will not be until his body goes into the grave, or the Lord comes in glory to "change our *vile body*, that it may be fashioned like unto His glorious body" (Philippians 3:21).

The remedy for a believer, in all things, is to know Christ.

YE ARE NOT YOUR OWN

(1 Corinthians 6:9)

Redeemed by Christ who died for me,
　　For Him 'tis now to live;
By grace divine from death made free,
　　To Christ the life I give:

In every action here below,
　　The Lord to sanctify;
The motive now in all I do—
　　His name to magnify.

One cherished sin within the heart,
　　One evil thought received,
The joy of Christ must needs depart,
　　His Holy Spirit grieved.

O Holy Spirit, have Thy way,
　　The power Thou must supply;
My heart and will I yield to Thee,
　　My God to glorify.

Chapter 14

VICTORY—THE LAW AND SIN

Thanks be to God, which giveth us the victory through our Lord Jesus Christ.—1 CORINTHIANS 15:57.

In what does this victory consist? Over what foes do we have the victory? In consists of final and complete triumph over all that opposes the spiritual life of the soul; a victory, a *glorious* victory over every foe. "Nay, in all these things, we are more than conquerors through Him that loved us" (Romans 8:37).

Oh, surely the redeemed soul would never separate any victory, any triumph in his spiritual life, any blessing received from God, from "Him that loved us." It is in Christ, and through Christ, and by Christ, and of Christ, and from Christ, all the way through, and into the ages of the ages. And so the prayer that the Holy Ghost would have each believing soul be uttering *now* with thankful humble heart to God, is found in Colossians 1:12 to 14—"Giving thanks unto the Father, which hath made us meet to be partakers of the inheritance of the saints in light: who hath delivered us from the power of darkness, and hath translated us into the kingdom of His dear Son; in whom we have redemption through His blood, even the forgiveness of sins."

Three things are presented by the Apostle in the verses from 1 Corinthians 15 over which he rejoices that believers have the victory. The law, sin, and death.

"The strength of sin is the law." Victory must therefore commence here. So long as the holy law of God condemns me, there can be no victory in anything. I cannot pray to God in faith until I know my sins are forgiven. I cannot love God, while I believe I am under His curse. I cannot serve God acceptably until I am justified by God. On the other hand, God cannot bless me while His law still condemns me. He cannot impart His Spirit to me, while guilt is yet upon me in His sight. To be made right legally in an absolute and entire release from every demand of the law, must be of necessity the first step in salvation. "Thanks be to God, who giveth us the victory through Jesus Christ our Lord." He "was delivered for our offences." He was "raised for our justification" (Romans 4:25).

"Put *my* where it says *our*, and read it again, slowly," was said to an anxious soul. *"I see it! I see it!"* was the happy response, after the request had been complied with. Reader, do *you* see it? If not, will you read the verse again. Read it slowly. Think what it means. Look to the Savior in His death as bearing the very sins you now feel to be condemning you. If Jesus Christ upon the Cross does not bring light to your soul, light will never come.

Do you not see from this verse, that the ground of your justification before God, the full and complete pardon of every sin, is simply the fact of Christ having died and satisfied God's law for you, and on your behalf?—and that you may know you are justified before God, in that He has raised Christ up from the dead to show you that He has accepted Him, and accepts you in Him?

A literal version has a beautiful translation of the verse, making this precious truth, of the believer's union with Christ in death and resurrection, perhaps more clear. It reads: "Who was delivered because of our offences, and was raised again because of our justification." Would we know the certainty of our justification from sin by God? We see it in the fact of His raising up Christ from the dead. The law is satisfied; its claims are vindicated. The sinner who accepts Christ as his Savior, is free. How can it be otherwise if, in the purpose of God, Christ was given to bear the penalty; and He has actually borne the penalty, and God has accepted the work as finished?

A story is told that, during our late sad War, a number of Southerners were arrested by a General of the Union Army, commanding a district in one of the border States, who tried them by court-martial, under the general charge of killing Union soldiers by shooting them from the bushes as they passed in small detachments through the country. They were all found guilty, and sentenced to be shot. After the sentence, the General allowed them to draw lots, and selected a few in this way for execution. Those selected by the fatal lot were to be shot the following morning. Tried, condemned, and waiting the execution of penalty, their condition was a sad one. Among the number thus waiting in despair, was a middle-aged man, a man of family, who was in deep distress at the fate that awaited him. During the evening a young man, a neighbor of the condemned, and one who had himself been of the number arrested but had escaped the fatal lot, came in and made the astonishing proposal to this man that he would take his place and die in his stead. He said, "I have no family to mourn my loss. I trust I am prepared to die; and I am willing, for the sake of your family, to die for you. The General says he will consent to the change, and accept my death in place of yours as satisfactory to the law."

The generous offer was accepted by the surprised and overcome man, and the substitute remained under guard until the morning came. With the morning, the young man was led out upon the parade-ground with his fellow-prisoners. A company of soldiers, with loaded guns, faced them, and at the command "Fire," he fell, his body riddled with bullets. Dead, under the penalty of law which he had voluntarily assumed for another. After the execution of the penalty, and the dead bodies had been taken away for burial, the remainder of the party, who had been held in arrest, were released and sent to their homes. Now, as the man, who was saved by the generous friend who thus died for him, enters his home and embraces the rejoicing wife and children who welcome him back to life again, what explanation will he give them as to his release from the penalty that hung over him? Doomed to death, what will he tell them was the means of his escape? Will he be talking about his convictions of danger, his fears, his repentance, his feeling bad, his tears, or anything of himself, as having anything to do with it? No, as the story goes, he certainly did nothing of the kind. He told them of the love of the young neighbor who offered to be his substitute: he told them of the mangled body that had filled the grave that had been dug for him; and that he lived because another had died in his place.

The writer has been informed that in the village graveyard near where this transaction occurred there is a grave with a head-stone bearing the name of this young hero, and an epitaph to his honor from the man for whom he died, acknowledging his debt of gratitude in that he died for him. Shall the believing sinner do less? Nay, shall he not do much more, rather, saved from eternal death by the death of Christ for him? How can he ever cease to love and praise? And how can he ever shrink from acknowledging his debt of gratitude to the Son of God, his Savior, "in whom we have redemption through His blood, the forgiveness of sins, according to the riches of His grace"? (Ephesians 1:7). This is the victory over the law in its condemning power. "Thanks be to God which giveth us the victory through our Lord Jesus Christ."

For the second aspect of victory, viz., *over sin*, look first at Romans 13:14—"But put ye on the Lord Jesus Christ, and make not provision for the flesh, to fulfil the lusts thereof." And then at Romans 6:11–14—"Likewise reckon ye also yourselves to be dead indeed unto sin, but alive unto God through Jesus Christ our Lord. Let not sin therefore reign in your mortal body, that ye should obey it in the lusts thereof. Neither yield ye your members as instruments of unrighteousness unto sin: but yield yourselves unto God, as those that are alive from the dead, and your members as instruments of righteousness unto God. For sin shall not have dominion over you: for ye are not under the law, but under grace." And lastly, at Romans 7:4—"Ye are become dead to the law by the body of Christ; that ye might be married to another, even to Him who was raised from the dead, that ye might bring forth fruit unto God."

In all of these references the central truth is—the spiritual union of the believing soul with a personal, living, risen Savior. The failure in overcoming sin begins, and is continued, because of failure to enter by faith into the enjoyment of this relationship. For peace of conscience as to my sins, I must see Christ on the cross, in His work of atonement. For power to overcome my sins, I must see Him as "the first-born from among the dead," the risen Head of His Church; and He, a living Savior, must dwell in my heart. If, in my knowledge of Christ, I stop at the cross, I cannot know His delivering power in my daily life.

The wonderful truth of Romans 7:4—showing the purpose of God, in setting the sinner free at the cross, to be the marriage of the sinner to Christ, as raised from the dead—is apprehended so feebly, that the power of Christ in His salvation is hardly known. Christ found His bride in prison, shut up under penalty of the law. He died to release her, that she then might marry Him. If the marriage is not consummated, how could the salvation be enjoyed? So far as He, the Bridegroom, is concerned, it is. He accepted us when we came to Him; for "Him that cometh to Me I will in no wise cast out." But, alas! His bride is very half-hearted, and slow to understand the fullness of His affection and the abundance of His power and grace for the supply of her every need. "Put *on* the Lord Jesus Christ." "Alive unto God *in* Jesus Christ."

"Married to Him who was raised from the dead." Surely, if we obeyed these exhortations, and accepted in simple faith the truth as to our standing before God in Christ, we should have victory over sin. The mistake is often made, that the actings of the flesh are the cause of the low spiritual life of believers. The truth is, that the low spiritual life of believers is the cause of the actings of the flesh. Let the soul come into a higher spiritual atmosphere, by being "married to Another;" let Christ be enjoyed and trusted, and fed upon through His Word; and the flesh is kept subdued. Engaged with Christ, the mind makes "no provision for the flesh," and it is kept under.

So that it is not by fighting our sins in detail that we get the victory—indeed, in this way, we find that the sins get the victory—but in coming into closer fellowship with Christ. Treat and trust Him, as a loving wife would trust her husband. As Ruth, the Moabitess—who found grace in the eyes of Boaz, and he became her redeemer and husband—trusted him to pay all her debts, and provide for all her needs. It would have grieved him, a mighty man of wealth, to have had her worried in the slightest degree about either.

Alas, how often we have grieved our blessed Lord by our doubts and suspicions as to whether He really *has* redeemed us from *all* our sins, or by unbelief as to the grace He has promised for *all* our need.

The exhortation of Romans 6:13, to *yield* ourselves unto

God, is very simple. Rebecca, the bride of Isaac, was asked the simple question, "Wilt thou go with this man?" And she said, "I will go."

Made alive in Jesus Christ, our risen Head, shall we not yield ourselves up to Him? The exhortation is based upon the truth of the 14TH verse, "For sin shall not have dominion over you, for (or, because) ye are not under law, but under grace." You are free from the dominion of the law of sin in your members, though not free from its existence.

The old slave-master, Sin, that has ruled you so long, has no right to claim your service further. Jesus Christ has purchased you. He is your Master—not sin. Yield yourself to Him. Assert your liberty; claim His protection. He will give it to you. He will sustain you; as you say, "In the name of the Lord Jesus, I am free. I will no longer yield, in this or that, wherein I have been in bondage. Lord Jesus, I yield to Thee."

The writer once witnessed a scene in Alabama that may help to illustrate this victory over the slave-master, Sin. A negro woman was brought before a Provost-marshal of the United States Army by an overseer, just as the war was closing in 1865, with the charge that she had tried to shoot him. United States soldiers filled the office, and gathered around to hear her story. It was simply this, which the overseer and two friends who accompanied him, admitted was substantially true.

The slaves had heard out on the plantation (some miles away from any point where troops had been) that the Northern Army had come, and that Abraham Lincoln had made them free. The overseer told them it was not true, and they were not free, and that they must work right on. She did work on, with the rest. But one day she learned that her little daughter, who had been sold to another plantation, was sick; and when she asked the overseer to let her go, he said No, she could not go. She told him that she believed she was free: that Abraham Lincoln had made her free; and she was going. She started down the lane; and he, obtaining his revolver, crossed the field, and, heading her off, pointed the revolver at her and told her to go back.

"Massa," said the woman, "I believed that Abraham Lincoln *had* made me free; and I just sprang at the overseer, and got him by the throat. He fell on his back, and I choked him until he got black, and begged; then I took his revolver and let him up, and pointed the pistol at him, and told him to go away, and let me alone. He went away; and I went to see my daughter, where these men found me, and brought me here."

The soldiers of Abraham Lincoln gave the woman three cheers for her faith in their President: and the officer who held his commission from Abraham Lincoln could do no other than say to the overseer, that under the authority of the United States Government he was bound to protect the woman with all the force at his command; and that he, and not the woman, was in a criminal position under existing law. The overseer was dismissed with a reprimand, and the poor woman left to rejoice in her freedom.

My brother, in your relations to the old master, Sin, whose law has once controlled you, go and do thou likewise. "Through this Man is preached unto you the forgiveness of sins: and by Him all that believe are justified from all things, from which ye could not be justified by the law of Moses" (Acts 13:38, 39).

Romans 5:8–10—"God commendeth His love toward us, in that, while we were yet sinners, Christ died for us. Much more then, being now justified by His blood, we shall be saved from wrath through Him. For if, when we were enemies, we were reconciled to God by the death of His Son, much more, being reconciled, we shall be saved by His life."

Shall a slave-woman believe the proclamation of man; and

will you not believe the proclamation of God? Shall she, inspired by faith in that proclamation, overcome her former master; and will not you, in the faith that Christ has redeemed you, overcome your old master? "Stand fast in the liberty wherewith Christ hath made you free."[1] Be assured that all the resources of the Almighty Savior are ready to support you, as you assert your liberty in the name of Jesus.

Burst the shackles, my brother. Throw off the yoke of bondage that any unlawful appetite or unhallowed lust has fastened upon you. Bring in faith to your living Savior your body to be filled with the Holy Spirit. Not in giving up one sin, this or that, do we get free; but in the yielding of ourselves to our new Master, in consecration to His blessed will, to "walk in the Spirit:" and in doing this we shall find that "he that abideth in Him sinneth not"—*i.e.,* is not sinning (1 John 3:6).

Thanks be to God that giveth us the victory through our Lord Jesus Christ!

The remedy in all things for a believer is to know Christ.

Ye Are Complete in Him

(Colossians 2:10)

Complete in Him: oh, precious word!
   May we by faith receive it;
That all our sins are put away
   Alone by Jesus merit.

Complete in Him while here below,
   With enemies contending;
His mighty power to daily know,
   From all our foes defending.

---

1 Galatians 5:1.

Complete in Him, though trials dark
    May often gather o'er us:
With faith and love we clasp the hand
    Of Him who goes before us.

Complete in Him for *all* things here,
    Where we the cross are bearing;
And soon for aye complete in Him,
    The crown we shall be wearing.

Chapter 15

VICTORY OVER DEATH

Thanks be to God, which giveth us the victory. 1 CORINTHIANS 15:57.

he last enemy that shall be destroyed is death."

"Death is swallowed up in victory."

"O death, where is thy sting? O grave, where is thy victory?" (1 Corinthians 15:26, 54, 55.)

So death is an enemy; always has been, and always will be; and is the last enemy to be destroyed. But, as an enemy, the believer is assured that in Christ he has the victory. With the question of sin settled, and judgment behind him at the Cross, instead of before him beyond the grave, the sting of death is removed; and the cause of its greatest terror, the fear of judgment, gone. Death no longer comes like a police officer to a believer, to bind him and take him to prison to await the great assize; but is allowed by God, as an enemy indeed, to hasten His children home—like a bad man who frightens the children as they come from school, and they run the faster to their father's house.

We have, as believers, the victory over death, in the triumph of our Savior in coming up from the grave. The victory there gained was a victory in which every believer has a share.

This robs the grave of its terror should we be called upon to lie therein. There is no question as to our coming up out of the grave. That was fully settled when He arose.

Sin cannot keep us there: for Christ took our sin and carried it to His grave, and God raised Him up above it all.

Satan cannot keep us there: for Christ by His death has overcome him that had the power of death; and He has the keys of death and the grave under His control. None can go in without His permission; and all must come forth when He shall speak the word.

Corruption cannot keep us there: for "this corruption must put on incorruption, and this mortal must put on immortality" (1 Corinthians 15:53).

So in Hebrews 2:15 we read, Christ came to "deliver them who, through fear of death, were all their life-time subject to bondage." In Philippians 1:21 the Apostle tells us—"For me to live is Christ, and to die is gain;" and in the 23RD verse—"having a desire to depart, and to be with Christ; which is far better." So in 2 Corinthians 5:8—"We are confident, I say, and willing rather to be absent from the body, and to be present with the Lord."

These words are unequivocal and plain. At death, the happy Spirit of the believer in Christ is with Christ in heaven. The same Lord Jesus, who was seen by the dying Stephen standing at the right hand of God when the heavens opened before him, and to whom he prayed, "Lord Jesus, receive my spirit!" will reveal Himself, and give dying grace to every one of His redeemed children, who may be called to follow Him into the grave; and their spirits shall rest with Him in conscious bliss in Paradise until the morning of the Resurrection, when they shall come with Him again to earth to be rehabilitated with re-created glorified bodies. "For if we believe that Jesus died and rose again, even so them also which sleep in Jesus will God bring with Him" (1 Thessalonians 4:14).

So if God call us to the high honor, as believers, of following Jesus even down into the grave, He will impart to us, in His grace, the same faith that He Himself had when He said, "Father, into Thy hands I commend my Spirit," and yielded His body to death, in the sure hope and certain expectation that God would raise Him up again.

So death to the believer is but the swinging open of the door through which he passes into the presence of his loving Lord. "Aren't you afeard, John," said the wife of a dying miner, as she bent over him in the last hour. "Afeard, lass?" said the man, "why should I be afeard? I ken Jesus; and Jesus kens me." And why should he fear? And why should any one who kens Jesus fear? "For He hath said, I will never leave thee, nor forsake thee: so that we may boldly say, The Lord is my helper, and I will not fear what man shall do unto me" (Hebrews 13:5, 6).

"I will never leave thee." Surely then, in the hour of death, He is there: and this should be our comfort, as those whom we love receive from us the last goodbye; and human affection and human care can go no farther. We simply resign our position that they may receive better care.

The last pressure of our hand is quickly followed by the clasp of His hand, who whispers, "Fear not, I will uphold thee." The last look of love from us is mingled with the tide of love that flows in upon them, in the consciousness that Jesus is near. The last sight of earthly friends is quickly succeeded by the rapturous vision of the glorified Lord. And as with them, so shall it be with us, if the Lord tarry, and we too fall asleep in Jesus.

How often have we known of dying saints, when lost to all consciousness and memory of things below, revive and smile at the name of Jesus! One of whom the writer knew, who made no sign of life as mother, husband, children came, and weeping said, "Do you know me?" whispered, in reply to the question, "Do you know Jesus?" *Precious Jesus, I know Him.* A poor Irish peasant woman, in dying, had closed her eyes, and the sister standing by, thinking her dead, commenced the wail of mourning, when the dying one whispered, "Hush, hark!" "What is it, Peggy?" said the sister. "You were disturbing me," was the reply. "I am listening to the breezes that are waving the branches of the Tree of Life." A few minutes more, and her spirit had fled.

What wonderful things have been suggested to us by the quick, strange, glad, awe-filled look of surprise that has come into the eyes of the dying saints! Some on battle-fields of carnage and blood, and some in homes of comfort and love, we have seen, as, lost to the sense of all earthly surroundings, they gave the far-away look at something unseen by those around; and have passed away. "Thanks be to God that giveth us the victory, through our Lord Jesus Christ."

So victory over death. Grace now given to meet it, and pass through it. The fear of it overcome; the sting of it removed; in the certain knowledge that this death is not penal in its character; not a visitation upon us of wrath against us for sin: for Christ hath taken that once for all, and "there is therefore now no condemnation to them which are in Christ Jesus." So it reads that Jesus died; and we, as believers, die in Him, as to penal death. And our dying, as to the separation of spirit and body for a little while, is called "falling asleep." "All things are yours," death included (1 Corinthians 3:21, 22).

Let the child of God just rest upon His unchanging Word for peace and comfort. If chosen to honor the Savior by bearing long-continued and severe pain of body; then by "all patience and long-suffering with joyfulness," let it be made manifest in you what His grace can do. And if the closing hours of life are

VICTORY OVER DEATH   121

darkened by special assaults of the adversary, even as were the last hours of our blessed Lord, and no gleams of glory seem to pierce the cloud, still trust and say, "This has been my comfort in my affliction; Thy Word hath quickened me."[1]

A dying saint who was passing through this experience at the close of a life that had been singularly free from doubt, and uniformly bright and happy in conscious fellowship with her Savior, said: "My faith is being tried. The brightness you speak of I do not have: but I have given my soul to Jesus; and I have learned in these years to know Him well enough to trust Him to put me to bed in the dark, if it be His will." These were God-honoring words of faith: more to the glory of the Lord Jesus than could be the relation of the happiest experience; for they honor His Word.

The further victory over death, as presented in the Scriptures—the final, complete, and glorious victory—is found in the presentation to the believer—as the blessed hope unto which he was saved (Romans 8:33, 24, *lit.*)—of the coming again from Heaven of our Lord Jesus; the resurrection of the sleeping bodies of the departed saints, and the changing of the bodies of the living ones "in a moment, in the twinkling of an eye, at the last trump" (1 Corinthians 15:52). "Behold, I show you a mystery, we shall not all sleep, but we shall all be changed" 1 Corinthians 15:51). "For this we say unto you by the Word of the Lord: that we that are alive, that are left unto the coming of the Lord, shall in no wise precede them that are fallen asleep. For the Lord Himself shall descend from Heaven, with a shout, with the voice of the archangel, and with the trump of God; and the dead in Christ shall rise first: then we that are alive, that are left, shall together with them be caught up in the clouds, to meet the Lord in the air: and so shall we ever be with the Lord" (1 Thessalonians 4:15–17 R.V.)

1 Psalm 119:50.

"Then shall be brought to pass the saying that is written—
Death is swallowed up in victory" (1 Corinthians 15:54).

Then, and not until then. Until that time "we that are in
this tabernacle do groan, being burdened: not for that we would
be unclothed (*i.e.,* die), but clothed upon; that mortality might
be swallowed up of life. Now He that hath wrought us for the
selfsame thing is God, who also hath given unto us the earnest
of the Spirit" (2 Corinthians 5:4, 5), and "ourselves also, which
have the firstfruits of the Spirit, even we ourselves groan within
ourselves, waiting for the adoption, to wit, the redemption of
our bodies" (Romans 8:23).

"For our citizenship (*revised version*) is in heaven: from
whence also we look for the Savior, the Lord Jesus Christ; who
shall change our vile body, that it may be fashioned like unto
His glorious body, according to the working whereby He is able
to subdue all things unto Himself" (Philippians 3:20, 21).

This will be PERFECTION: perfection of bliss, perfection of
holiness, perfection of happiness, perfection of attainment: the
realization of all for which we were redeemed; and of which
we now have the firstfruits in the indwelling of the Spirit in
our souls, "which is the earnest of our inheritance until the
redemption of the purchased possession, unto the praise of His
glory" (Ephesians 1:14). For this we are commanded to *wait*—
"waiting for the adoption" (Romans 8:23); "looking for that
blessed hope, and the glorious appearing of the great God and
our Savior Jesus Christ" (Titus 2:13). To *expect*—"For the earnest expectation of the creature waiteth for the manifestation of
the sons of God" (Romans 8:19). To *desire*—"Earnestly desir-
ing to be clothed upon with our house which is from Heaven"
(2 Corinthians 5:2). To *pray for*—"Even so, come, Lord Jesus"
(Revelation 22:20).

We are told to watch, for in such an hour as we think not

He will come (Matthew 24:42, 44). We do not watch for death. Death is *not* our blessed hope. Death is "departing to be with Christ," a "falling asleep," as in Scripture terms. The coming of the Lord is His personal presence with us; the awaking of those that sleep.

Oh, may the young convert receive this truth fully into his soul; and be of the number of those that wait for their Lord, when He will return from the wedding; "that, when He cometh and knocketh, they may open unto Him immediately! Blessed are those servants whom the Lord, when He cometh, shall find watching" (Luke 12:36, 37).

The coming of Jesus again to this earth; the personality and imminence of that coming; the glory following that coming for His saints; and the woe and disaster for those who have despised and rejected God's grace—constitute the most prominent theme of the Scriptures. May the Holy Spirit unfold the meaning of these Scriptures to the reader; and may his heart enter fully into all that God has been pleased to reveal of His glorious purposes concerning Christ and His Church! "Yet a little while; and He that shall come will come, and will not tarry" (Hebrews 10:37).

Oh, what a victory the believer will then realize! Despised and persecuted, he may have been on earth, one "of whom the world was not worthy,"[1] defamed, laughed at, and made as the offscouring of all things: sorely beset by Satan through his earthly pilgrimage: hated and opposed by the world: long chained to a body of humiliation, in which he groaned and toiled, sinned and repented, suffered and battled against: hating sin, and humbled by its presence: loving God, and loathing self; and self clinging to him. But now the hour has struck; the trumpet sounds; the great deliverance has come; the dragon is cast into the pit; "the kingdom of the world is become the kingdom of

1 Hebrews 11:38.

our Lord and of His Christ,"[1] and, as a part of the Lord's Christ, He stands upon the sea of glass in His glorified, immortal, and sinless body; and as a redeemed spirit in a redeemed body, reigning with the Lord of glory over a redeemed earth, He joins in the song of the ransomed host described by John in Revelation 19:6: "And I heard as it were the voice of a great multitude; and as the voice of many waters; and as the voice of mighty thunderings: saying, Alleluia! for the Lord God Omnipotent reigneth."

Thanks be to God which giveth us the victory through our Lord Jesus Christ. Therefore, my beloved brethren, be ye stedfast, unmoveable, always abounding in the work of the Lord, forasmuch as ye know that your labour is not in vain in the Lord.—1 CORINTHIANS 15:57, 58.

THERE'S A GLORIOUS KINGDOM WAITING

There's a glorious Kingdom waiting
In he land beyond the sky,
Where the saints have been gathering year by year;
And the days are swiftly passing
That shall bring the Kingdom nigh,
For the coming of the Kingdom draweth near.
With the coming of the Kingdom
We shall see our glorious Lord,
For the King, ere the Kingdom, must appear.
Hallelujah to His name,
Who redeemed us by His blood!
Oh, the coming of the Kingdom draweth near.
'Tis the hope of yonder Kingdom,
And the glory there prepared,
And the looking for the Saviour to appear,

---

1 Revelation 11:15.